AF424245

Weathering the Storms

Weathering the Storms

Deepak M. Babu

Copyright © 2025 by Deepak M. Babu

All rights reserved. This book or any portion thereof may not be reproduced or used in any manner whatsoever without the express written permission of the author except for the use of brief quotations in a book review.

Scripture quotations are taken from the New Revised Standard Version Updated Edition. Copyright © 2021 National Council of Churches of Christ in the United States of America. Used by permission. All rights reserved worldwide.

First Printing, 2025

Email me at: deepakmbabu@gmail.com

My YouTube handle: https://www.youtube.com/@deepakmbabu

I blog at purposescrossed.blog and acutelyobtuse.blog

Cover art by Mercy Kurian (Instagram handle: teal_and_ochre)

In memoriam

Alice Deepak Babu

This started with you.

But never shall this walk end

Though you've gone ahead

For Mercy

A better sister,

A friend through life's toughest vales

No one could ask for

Table of Contents

Preface

The reader may be wondering why there is a need for yet another book on the Sermon on the Mount. Hasn't this part of the Gospel according to Matthew been studied and written about endlessly? What could another book on this Sermon contribute to the Church?

In this book, while I have written in a devotional style, I have incorporated a lot of scholarship. Hence, the devotions will not scratch the surface but will actually delve deep into the text of the Sermon. I have always believed that the common disjunction between the heart and the head is ridiculous for humans who have both. Hence, I believe it is in this merger that this book offers something unique.

The Sermon on the Mount has been a favorite of mine over the years. With each reading I find myself growing and learning something new. Hence, I do not offer these devotions with the claim that I have said anything final on any part of the Sermon. Rather, these devotions represent my ongoing wrestling with these three chapters of the first Gospel.

When I say ongoing, it may come as a surprise to some readers that I began this endeavor in the summer of 2001! Yes, it has taken that long for this book to receive this shape. Some of the devotions had to be modified to accommodate my more current understandings of those parts of the Sermon. Others needed a very heavy redo. Still others had to be completely trashed and started afresh. Of course, I realized that the continuous editing would serve no one. Hence, I decided to put an end to that process at the end of May 2025, leaving myself the first half of June 2025 to proofread the manuscript.

I am grateful to my sister, Mercy, for the excellent cover art. Her contributions to many of my books has been exceptional and I have dedicated this book to her.

The impetus for this series of devotions came from my late wife, Alice. When I started as Cell Pastor (no, this is not a prison role) at North University Park Church, LA, one of the things I wanted to do was produce material that could be used to mentor people in the way of Jesus. I had narrowed it down to the Farewell Discourse in the Gospel according to John, the "Love" chapter – 1 Corinthians 13, and the Sermon. It was Alice who suggested that I tackle the Sermon since it was directly about Jesus telling his disciples the kind of lives they should be leading. I just wish I had decided to put an end to the editing process while she was still alive. I'm sure she would have loved to see it in print.

At the same time, I have to admit that a lot of the previously mentioned heavy redoing and trashing came in the wake of her death as I wrestled to make sense of the absolutely good Father that Jesus portrays in the Sermon in light of the pain and suffering she endured. Nothing that could not withstand the claim that God is good in light of, and not despite, what Alice went through could be admitted in the final version.

Introduction

The Sermon on the Mount contains gems that, unfortunately, have been lost to centuries of inappropriate and misguided theologizing. Since there are only a few translation issues in this part of Matthew's Gospel, I have not prepared a translation. Rather, I will follow the NRSVUE and, whenever I disagree with it, I will indicate it in the appropriate devotion. The difficulties with the Sermon on the Mount do not primarily lie in translation, but with our unwillingness to take Jesus seriously.

The Sermon on the Mount is probably one of the best-known segments of teaching in all the ancient texts. And it is easily the most misunderstood. The reason for this is that the text is distant from those of us who live in the 21st century. The text is written in *koine* Greek, which no one speaks today. It was written in and to a culture quite foreign to the ones we live in. It references cultural and political situations that are unfamiliar to us. Moreover, most likely Jesus spoke in Aramaic. So even the Greek text is a translation of what he said! And as anyone who is fluent in multiple languages knows, something is always lost in the act of translation.

Yet, according to the Gospel of Matthew, the Sermon

on the Mount is Jesus' first sustained teaching discourse, coming soon after his baptism, temptation, and the calling of his disciples. Having been given this position in the Gospel, it has a programmatic role, enabling us to understand the ministry of Jesus as a whole. Hence, in order to understand Jesus, it is crucial that we understand the Sermon on the Mount. However, it is my opinion that the Sermon on the Mount has too much theological baggage attached to it, with many common views not even bothering to reflect the original situation within which Jesus spoke these words.

In this series of devotions, we will look at the Sermon on the Mount in detail. I will draw from many giants of the faith, both past and present, and will distill this learning into these short devotion segments. I am not infallible. But then, neither are my sources! But I will be genuinely wrestling with the scriptures and will present my understanding in these devotions. I believe that even my sources, and especially those with whom I have serious disagreement have wrestled with the scriptures honestly *coram deo* - that is, in the presence of God. So, my disagreements with anyone should not be taken in any way as an indictment of those with whom I disagree, though I often express bewilderment at some conclusions that others have reached.

Before we begin with the devotions, let us state some hermeneutical principles. First, no interpretation that is unthinkable in the mouth of a first century Galilean Jew can be accepted. While Jesus certainly challenged long cherished perspectives on the relationship of humans with God, he did not do it without a context. And he was a first century Galilean Jew. Second, no interpretation that renders God unfaithful to his promises can be accepted. The bible goes to great lengths to insist on our being able to trust God because he is completely faithful. Hence, any view that questions God's faithfulness is to be treated with due suspicion.

Third, Jesus, through Matthew, should be allowed the full use of normal human language. Human languages have not changed since the first century at least as far as the breadth of expressions they are capable of communicating is concerned. If we use metaphor, so did Jesus. If we use similes, so did he. He should be allowed the full use of rhetorical devices like hyperbole, sarcasm, merism, synecdoche, etc. There are other principles that I could mention, but these are crucial because they impact our view of the humanness of Jesus, the faithfulness of God, and the historicity of revelation. And so, with that out of the way, we can begin with our devotions on the Sermon on the Mount.

Week 1

Week 1, Day 1: Matthew 5.1

When Jesus saw the crowds, he went up the mountain, and after he sat down, his disciples came to him.

One of Matthew's main purposes is to show Jesus as the new Moses promised in <u>Deuteronomy 18.15</u>. Of course, Matthew wants the reader to believe that Jesus was *more* than what Moses imagined. However, in Matthew's view, Jesus certainly wasn't *less*!

So here Jesus, like Moses, goes up a mountain. The parallel between Moses, who ascended to receive the Torah from Yahweh, and Jesus, who ascended this mountain to give a new Torah to his disciples is striking. But as the previous sentence makes clear, while Moses was the recipient of the divine instruction, Jesus was the source of it.

Matthew also includes the intriguing point that Jesus sat down. We do not read about Moses sitting down when he went up the mountain. Contrary to what we are used to, in ancient Jewish society a teacher sat while teaching. (cf. <u>Luke</u>

4.20) Sitting communicated a position of authority. This is true in India as well. If an elder enters the room, many of us would stand to show them honor and take our seats only after they have taken their seat.

Interestingly, Matthew does not tell us that Jesus called the disciples to him. Rather, as soon as they saw that he had taken a seat, they knew he was going to start teaching. The only appropriate response was to approach the teacher and receive the important instruction directly from him. This parallels the ascent up the mountain of the leaders of Israel. (Exodus 24) Just as at Mount Sinai the representatives of Israel went up the mountain to meet with God, so also here, the representatives of the new Israel went up this mountain to meet with Jesus.

The stage is now set. The teacher has taken a seat. The disciples have approached him and have gathered around him, ready to receive wisdom from him. What will he now say? What wisdom will he be giving them for this new Israel? And just as Moses began with the short and memorable Ten Commandments, so also Jesus will begin with a series of short and memorable sayings. But where he begins is surprising, as we will see tomorrow.

And he began to speak and taught them, saying: "Blessed[1] are the poor in spirit, for theirs is the kingdom of heaven."[2]

Jesus begins his great Sermon with an indication that he will be challenging what we accept as true. To a world that values riches, to a church that idolizes spiritual giants, Jesus elevates those who are poor and poor in spirit. These are the ones who now possess God's kingdom and who are promised it in the future. Riches lull us into feeling secure. But whatever gives us our security is our god. This is why Jesus blesses the poor—not because they are poor, but because their situation enables them to trust God for his provision.

---

[1] The Greek word *makarios* translated "blessed" carries the notion that the person designated as *makarios* is the privileged recipient of divine favor. The emphasis falls not on the state of the person but on the fact that God's favor is directed toward the person because of their state.

[2] The phrase "kingdom of heaven" is another way of saying "kingdom of God" and it refers to that realm—not necessarily physical, but not merely spiritual either—in which God's will is done. In Matthew the phrase "kingdom of heaven" is used rather than "kingdom of God" so as not to offend the sensibilities of those who use circumlocutions while referring to God.

The bible witnesses to the fact that God has a special concern for those who are poor, those who are disenfranchised. We often forget this in our quest for power and wealth. Even in the church! We look for signs of spiritual power and believe that God blesses financially those who are truly spiritual. However, Jesus elevates exactly the opposite. But we often obscure this by spiritualizing Jesus' words. We say that Jesus is blessing those who recognize their spiritual need and their inability to save themselves.

But is that really what Jesus is saying? Remember, Jesus is talking to his disciples. They are already a part of God's people! They are the ones who later can be blessed for being persecuted for Jesus' name's sake.

The phrase "poor in spirit" could quite easily refer to those who, in the estimation of the recognized spiritual authorities, are poor—that is, lacking in true spirituality. This is how many Jews viewed the followers of Jesus because Jesus' followers did not observe many of the religious norms of the Jews. This also makes sense of why Jesus addresses many of these norms in the sermon. Jesus is blessing his followers, who are being accused of having fake spirituality.

The issue of fake spirituality is still relevant. Do we not still evaluate the spiritual depth of other Christians even today? Jesus might now bless those whom we think are spiritually shallow! The spiritually rich people have labeled them spiritual paupers. These people are perceived to have no "spiritual bank account" on which to rely. They can depend only on God's favor. The wondrous thing is that Jesus tells us that these people are recipients of God's favor.

Week 1, Day 3: Matthew 5.4

"Blessed are those who mourn, for they will be comforted."

"Laugh and others will laugh with you; cry and you will cry alone." We are all too aware of the truth behind this aphorism. When we are up, when things are going well, people might even flock to us. However, when faced with tragedy, most often we are left to fend for ourselves. Yet, it is precisely those who are mourning that Jesus blesses with comfort.

We should observe that Jesus does not restrict the blessing to certain types of mourning or certain reasons for mourning. The blessing is all encompassing, including everyone who has felt, who now feels, or who will feel that this world is not as it was meant to be. Here we must be clear that mourning is not some passing feeling of dissatisfaction or frustration that one experiences when, for instance, one misses a bus or is caught in a traffic jam. Neither can we say we are mourning when we stand to benefit from whatever supposedly causes our tears.

For instance, we do not truly mourn the death of a loved one, if we are simultaneously planning how to enjoy whatever the deceased person has bequeathed us. To truly mourn is to be willing to reverse the circumstances if we had the power, while acknowledging that we do not have such power.

Now, Jesus' blessing is in the passive voice. This keeps the identity of the person who does the comforting secret. In the bible, the passive voice is often used to indicate divine action. While this could be a way to avoid using God's name, this does not seem to be Jesus' intent. After all, Jesus is able to address God as his Father. Why then would he need to use the passive voice to avoid mentioning God directly? More probable is that he uses the passive voice precisely because of the ambiguity inherent in it. The hearers are left with some uncertainty about the identity of the comforter.

The effect of this is explosive. If I insist that God does the comforting though Jesus does not mention God, I can never be sure that God will not use me to comfort someone who mourns. Furthermore, if I am in mourning, I cannot preclude God's using another human to comfort me. Indeed, it is most likely that Jesus uses the passive voice because God uses humans to comfort humans. Since we are creatures created to be God's image, God most often does his work in and through humans. We are the ones who are given the privilege to be God's voice and hands for those who are desperately in need of divine comfort. And conversely, when we are in need of divine comfort, God will give other humans the privilege of being his voice and hands for us.

Of course, we could remember that Jesus is the 'man of sorrows'. If, then, we believe he comforts us because he is acquainted with sorrow, we must also realize that God can comfort others through us because we are acquainted with sorrow. Christians who take suffering as a sign of divine displeasure are, therefore, excluding themselves from being either agents or recipients of this blessing. But perhaps the only comfort we will receive is the knowledge that God will redeem our sorrows not by taking away our wounds and pain, but by using our sorrows for the healing of others. Perhaps this beatitude is trying to teach us that the only healers are wounded healers, the only comforters, mourning comforters.

Week 1, Day 4: Matthew 5.5

"Blessed are the meek, for they will inherit the earth."

This beatitude is a development of <u>Psalm 37.11</u>. The word translated "meek" is the same one Jesus uses to describe himself in <u>Matthew 11.29</u> when he says, "I am *gentle* and humble in heart." Meekness, we can conclude, has something to do with being gentle and humble. Gentleness is the opposite of forcefulness and violence. To treat another person gently is to refuse to force that person or to violate that person. But gentleness is relational, which means that a gentle person of necessity must interact with others. Humility is the opposite of pride or arrogance. To be humble is to refuse to exalt oneself—especially at the expense of another.

But at the same time, humility is not self-effacement. To be humble is not to put down oneself but to refuse to raise oneself, especially at the expense of another person. It is to have and communicate a healthy and accurate appraisal of oneself. Hence, Jesus can be said to be humble even though he quite clearly said things that are far from self-effacing like, "I am the resurrection and the life." In other words, even though he made grand claims about himself, we can consider him to be humble *because* the claims were true concerning him. Never once does Jesus speak of himself in a derogatory manner. Nor does he allow anyone else to do the same.

Therefore, Jesus is not pronouncing a blessing on people who beat up on themselves. He is not advocating that Christians should be doormats. While a doormat can do nothing when people trample it, a meek person can make decisions. The decisions will stem from a strong conviction of his or her dignity and value in the eyes of God. A meek person can choose to allow others to deny him or her common human rights. A meek person, on the other hand, can also demand that justice be done. The course of action will depend on how the decision will affect the other person.

In other words, a meek person will not act out of selfish motives. Such selfless action can only come from the security one has in being a child of God. And to such children Jesus promises the earth.

This promise is yet to be realized. Jesus promises it as a future hope to those who, while imitating him, are trodden under and denied a share in God's gift that is the earth. God has given the earth to all humans. God will give it as an inheritance to those who follow Jesus and have no place to lay their heads.

It bears pausing here to remind ourselves that Jesus promises the meek people that they will inherit *the earth*. The 'destiny' of humans is not some ethereal, spiritual realm, call it 'heaven' if you will. Rather, we have been created for and are promised to inherit *the earth*. All ideas such as 'this world is not my home' or 'I'm just passing through', etc. deny the blessing that God has kept for those who follow his example as demonstrated in the life and work of Jesus.

Meekness and trust are also two sides of one coin. When we trust Yahweh and find our security in him, we will not join the rat race in which others are involved. We will not define success as the world does. We will march to the beat of a different drummer. We will define success as emulating Jesus—the one who is gentle and humble.

Week 1, Day 5: Matthew 5.6

"Blessed are those who hunger and thirst for justice,[3] for they will be filled."

Most of us are familiar with hunger and thirst, some obviously to a greater extent than others. We can make two important observations about these cravings. First, they are natural and automatic. None of us has ever had to train our bodies to become hungry or thirsty. Rather, hunger and thirst come upon us involuntarily. Second, they are repetitive. We never eat with the expectation that the meal will suffice for the rest of our lives. Rather, we know that, in a few hours, we will hunger and thirst again for food and drink.

In employing the images of hunger and thirst, Jesus tells us that our desire for justice is to become second nature to us until we need to expend no energy to summon the desire. Moreover, the desire is to be repetitive. One moment of justice should remind us that we would need another moment shortly.

---

[3] As has been my practice, I have translated *dikaiosúnē* as 'justice' instead of 'righteousness' to emphasize the major thrust of the equivalent Hebrew words *tzedakah*, which is what Jesus most likely would have used.

However, what is this justice for which we are to hunger and thirst? As mentioned in the footnote, the Greek word here is *dikaiosúnē*, which is most often translated as 'righteousness'. Now, there are two ways of considering what 'righteousness' might mean. First, if we think of righteousness in legal terms as being a right standing before God, then Jesus' beatitude makes no sense. After all, with such a view, we cannot desire a right standing before God until we already have it, in which case it is of no consequence to desire it! Just as the prodigal son was always the father's son, even when *he* himself had undermined the relationship, so also a person who has 'come to his/her senses' and now hungers for a right standing before God is only being awoken to the fact that the relationship *never* was broken. Unfortunately, we have too often heard righteousness described in legal terms. This makes us predisposed to taking a route that makes Jesus someone who speaks nonsensical words.

Second, we can understand 'righteousness' in terms of relationships. In such a view, 'righteousness' would entail doing what is best for a given relationship. This eschews the notion that discipleship consists in observing some universal principles. Rather, we are to struggle to determine what might be best for a particular relationship in a given situation—especially when other relationships also vie for our attention.

For instance, what must I do if securing an important business contract depends on my working late on my twenty-fifth wedding anniversary? Should I attend my friend's funeral or my niece's graduation? Life hurls at us one such predicament after another. Relating rightly is not easy. That is why Jesus asks us to train ourselves so that what is not easy would become second nature.

According to this view, rather than concentrate on our personal purity, a result of understanding 'righteousness' in legal terms, we are to earnestly desire wholesome relationships. When we do so, Jesus promises us that we will be filled. This does not mean that others will relate to us in wholesome ways. Rather, Jesus promises the satisfaction of knowing that we have treated others the way God treats them.

However, as noted, I have translated *dikaiosúnē* as 'justice'. 'Justice' involves not just doing what is right for the other person in the context of a relationship. Rather, 'justice' also involves making reparations for past infractions. While 'righteousness' might only be concerned about the present, 'justice' attempts to make redressal for past injustices as well. It is more holistic than 'righteousness' and, hence, is likely what Jesus had in mind for this beatitude.

Week 1, Day 6: Matthew 5.7

"Blessed are the merciful, for they will receive mercy."

In the previous devotion, we saw that Jesus blesses those who desire wholesome relationships and those who enact justice for others. In case we spend too much energy deciding what would constitute right ways of relating or what justice might look like, Jesus gives us a clue. Jesus blesses those who are merciful.

Mercy is inherently relational. This should indicate that the righteousness Jesus has in mind is not individual, legal, right standing, but relational. One could say that mercy helps us understand the meaning of righteousness. I may not claim to be righteous while at the same time being merciless.

Mercy also cannot exist without a past injustice. I can show another person mercy only when, having been treated badly by the other person, I now find that the tables have been turned and that I have some power over the other person.

We can be merciful in two ways. On the one hand, we can refuse to get even with someone who has hurt us. On the other hand, we could bless someone without his or her earning our blessing. Both are expressions of mercy. While in one instance mercy might be expressed through restraint, in another it might be realized through lavishness. In the case in which someone has hurt us, the very notion of 'getting even' implies that we have already been disadvantaged by the other person. In the case in which we unilaterally bless someone, giving that person something implies our not being able to use whatever we give.

In both cases, we choose the position of being disadvantaged. The willingness—or rather the choice—to be disadvantaged might be the hallmark of mercy.

Jesus blesses those who are merciful, saying, "They will receive mercy." As we saw in the devotion on Matthew 5.4, the passive voice reflects the fact that, though God may be the source of the blessing, he uses humans to carry out his work. With respect to this beatitude, God is certainly the fount of mercy. At the same time, he uses humans to demonstrate his mercy.

Unfortunately, Jesus' blessing does not guarantee that, if we are merciful to others, others will be merciful to us. Mercy, after all, is not mercy if it is coerced! Those of us who find our merciful ways are rarely reciprocated may have to wait to receive mercy from God's hand alone.

Having heard the beatitude, however, we cannot ignore the implications it has for us. If we say that we are God's people, then we have no excuse for refusing to act in accordance with God's will. And Jesus tells us that God's will is to be merciful to those who are merciful. It follows then that, through this beatitude, Jesus is summoning us to be God's agents of mercy, primarily as initiators of mercy, but also in response to those whom we perceive as agents of mercy. In this way, contrary to the cycle of violence and unforgiveness that characterizes relationships - individual or communal - in the world, we can be agents who initiate a new kind of cycle, one that will lead to the healing of the nations.

Week 1, Day 7: Matthew 5.8

"Blessed are the pure in heart, for they will see God."

In Exodus 33.20 Yahweh tells Moses, "You cannot see me, for no human being can see me and survive." Yet, in the sixth beatitude Jesus promises those who are pure in heart that they will see God. What do we make of this? In what way is the beatitude valid and how does it relate to the words of Yahweh to Moses?

One way of approaching this is to see the words to Moses as primary, indicating that Jesus is speaking of our *aiōnial*[4] state when we will be pure and when we will see God face to face. This has been a common approach. However, it results in Jesus teaching the obvious! Of course, we will see God face to face in the new creation! Jesus would hardly then be a rabbi worth following. No one needs a teacher who just regurgitates the obvious!

Another way of approaching this is to say that Moses

---

[4] As has been my practice, I have left the word *aiōnios* untranslated. It is normally translated as 'eternal', which only leads to more confusion in my opinion.

was, like all of us, impure, but that purity can be achieved. This approach of purgation has also been common, not least among those who have misunderstood the mystics' desire for the beatific vision as something obtained in response to one's own purity. The mystics, however, did not seek the beatific vision as something they would earn and that God would grant them for their superior purity. Rather, the mystics sought the beatific vision knowing that it would be a sign that they had purified themselves. A twisting of the goals of the mystics, however, is quite common in Protestant circles where it is seen as a way of working for salvation. However, the whole thrust of the Sermon on the Mount—and Jesus' ministry—warns against such striving. The mystics understood this.

A third option suggests that 'pure in heart' means 'single-minded devotion' and that Jesus is blessing those who are focused on God. However, the first part of the beatitude does not mention God! In fact, none of these approaches takes into account the context of the beatitude. And this is why they miss the point, though the third option comes close.

So, what does the context tell us? The beatitude lies between the blessing on the merciful and the blessing on the peacemakers. This should give us some clue as to what 'pure in heart' means. It must be somewhat related to 'mercy' and 'peace' or else there would be no reason for Jesus' including it where he did. Going with the third option mentioned above, 'single-minded devotion' might be a correct way of rendering 'pure in heart'. However, in keeping with the context, it is best to think of the devotion as being about 'forgiveness' or 'reconciliation'. These are related to both mercy and peace and, therefore, make better sense.

Moreover, given the way Jesus ends his model prayer in 6.14-15—an admonishment we too easily forget when praying—it would seem that it is in forgiving others that we will get that beatific vision—though not necessarily in the same manner or with the same content as often supposed. We often assume that God is to be seen in the big things. However, as many of Jesus' parables tell us, and as Jesus' life itself indicates, God is most present in the small things—the little events in which his people dare to act like him.

Week 2

Week 2, Day 1: Matthew 5.9

"Blessed are the peacemakers, for they will be called children of God."

In the previous devotion, we saw that there is a movement of thought in the beatitudes. Jesus has consistently been intensifying the yardstick of discipleship. However, we often think the beatitudes are unrelated to each other and lose Jesus' thrust. Now it is no longer merely a matter of being considered spiritually poor (v. 3), or of showing mercy (v. 7), or even of having a single focus on forgiveness (v. 8). Now Jesus would have us enter a conflict not our own and be agents of peace.

This is a tall order for sure. However, we do not get out of this predicament by assuming that Jesus was speaking figuratively. We cannot let the title 'Prince of Peace' that we use of Jesus to be the excuse for leaving all the peacemaking to him. After all, he does bless those who make peace. And he certainly was not going around pronouncing blessings on himself!

We should also look at the blessing Jesus mentions. While the 'pure in heart' will see God, the peacemakers are promised membership in God's family! Children of God will quite obviously see God. But what they have in addition to this vision is free access to God, just as children have free access to parents. Intensification of discipleship results in intensification of the promise.

This should give us pause when we try to appropriate promises of scripture. If we interpret the condition of the promise figuratively—here by assuming that Jesus is talking about some nebulous 'spiritual' peace—then we are left with only a figurative promise—here that we are not really children of God but that Jesus is using some kind of linguistic flourish.

What Jesus is calling for are disciples who will go to the extent he did to make peace. It is a tall order indeed. We find it hard enough to be forgiving in our personal conflicts. How much more difficult it is to understand both sides of another conflict and persuade the parties concerned to be reconciled! So often, we listen only to one side of a conflict and try to help only to see our efforts merely exacerbate the conflict. Only by understanding all sides will we be able to work toward a lasting peace.

Moreover, understanding alone is not enough. As a teacher, I am quite fed up with people saying that 'knowledge is power' or that the problem is a 'lack of education'. The Nazi genocide of the minorities, including the Jews, was done by a people group who were very highly educated. And today the genocide of the Palestinians is being done by supposedly well-educated nations. Education and knowledge are great. But education and knowledge alone never liberate.

Rather, without a heart that includes all creation, including all humans, education and knowledge will only facilitate the injustices those with power inflict on those who are powerless. In order to be those who make peace in the world, we must reject the parochialism that most of our leaders feed us with. We must reject any idea that considers any human as lesser than we are, no matter what the qualifying trait(s) is/are. We must be willing to say that peace between humans created by God is far more important than our own lives. And we must be willing to act this way. For it is the way of Jesus. It is the way to imitate God. It is how we truly experience what it means to have God as our Father. It is how we experience God's embrace!

Week 2, Day 2: Matthew 5.10

"Blessed are those who are persecuted for the sake of justice,[5] for theirs is the kingdom of heaven."

As has been the case with the other beatitudes, this one has been interpreted in an individualistic manner. We have assumed that, when Jesus mentions 'righteousness', he means our personal piety, purity, and sinlessness. Then we assume we are being persecuted for righteousness' sake when someone ridicules us for some practice that stems from our faith related convictions.

However, this could hardly be any further from Jesus' point! All along in the beatitudes, he has been speaking about relational characteristics. He has moved from people's perception of us, to our response and attitude. He has heightened the quality of discipleship with each beatitude till in v. 9 he blesses those who would choose to become mediators of peace. Now he tells us what to expect when we do this.

---

[5] As has been my practice, I have translated *dikaiosúnē* as 'justice' instead of 'righteousness' to emphasize the major thrust of the equivalent Hebrew words *tzedakah*, which is what Jesus most likely would have used.

Conflicts often exist because someone stands to gain from them. Drawing upon the principle of 'divide and conquer', colonialists of the past, pitted tribes against each other, thereby making it easy for the invaders to defeat the natives. In such a situation, those who would try to reconcile the warring parties would face bitter reprisals from the invaders. Those who work to heal relationships will often be accused of ulterior motives by those who stand to gain from the brokenness of the relationship. If you have ever played the role of peacemaker, you will know that I am speaking the truth.

However, in the devotion on Matthew 5.6, we saw that Jesus was most likely talking about hungering and thirsting for justice. Peacemaking cannot be engaged in without the intention to bring about justice, which will involve the attempt to make redressal for past injustices. When we try to do this, those who perpetrated past injustices will be called to make reparations for their past actions. This is not something they will willingly do. And if they are still in a position of power, they will likely act out in wrath against those who would want them to set things right.

This is what Jesus is warning us about. When we work to reconcile people in conflict, we are working to heal their relationship. We are attempting to make them relate rightly with each other. We are working for the cause of 'righteousness' and 'justice'. When we do so, we should expect some people to obstruct us and even to harm us. It is easy, in the context of a relationship that is already strained, to make either or both parties suspect the person who is trying to heal the relationship. And this is why being a person who works to promote right relatedness is often a thankless job.

But Jesus blesses the person who is reviled in the cause of reconciliation. For the second time in the beatitudes, he pronounces the blessing 'theirs is the kingdom of heaven'. Such people, by virtue of their reconciliatory work and the willingness to persist in that work despite harsh opposition, show themselves already to live in that realm in which God's will is done. And the stubborn determination to remain God's peacemakers in the face of life-threatening adversity is what Jesus blesses.

"Blessed are you when people revile you and persecute you and utter all kinds of evil against you falsely on my account. Rejoice and be glad, for your reward is great in heaven, for in the same way they persecuted the prophets who were before you."

Jesus introduces two remarkable changes here. First, till now the beatitudes have described characteristics in third person—"the poor in spirit," "those who mourn," "the meek," etc. Now Jesus forcefully switches to the second person. Second, it is in this beatitude that Jesus inserts himself explicitly with the words "on my account" (NRSV) or "because of me" (NIV).

Suddenly the focus of the beatitudes is on those who hear them. No longer can the listener remain at a distance. Some of Jesus' disciples may have been thinking, for instance, "Sure, those who mourn are blessed, but, Jesus, you can count me out of that blessing." We too react in similar ways. Otherwise, why would we support various kinds of violence when Jesus blesses peacemakers? Why would we clamor for success when Jesus blesses the meek? Why do we seek retribution—even legally permitted retribution—when Jesus blesses those who show mercy? Such attitudes reveal the lie we live—we really do not think Jesus is addressing us!

But Jesus, like a good Hebrew prophet (e.g. Amos 1-2), allows his hearers to initially remain at a distance, possibly cheering Jesus' "good insights." Then he moves the focus on his audience. And they realize too late that all the beatitudes were about them. They are the ones expected to accept the invitation to be "poor in spirit," "merciful," "meek," etc. Moreover, they are the ones who are to be "peacemakers," calling down on themselves the wrath of others to the extent that they are "persecuted for righteousness' sake." But in so doing, they will be persecuted because of Jesus!

No longer can we entertain the illusion that the beatitudes are universal principles. Rather, they are specific blessings for the people of God, for those who follow Jesus in God's reconciliatory work. God has always wanted a people who would partner with him to spread his redemptive work throughout the world. Unfortunately, we have often thought of being God's people solely in terms of receiving blessings and gifts from God rather than in terms of being called to serve others. However, by directing his focus on the listeners and including himself at the center of this beatitude, Jesus does not allow us to have a view that God's people only receive blessings. Rather, they are called to be blessings to others.

Now Jesus does not have in mind some mild or generic kind of opposition. He is describing the harshest form of opposition that we could face in the course of following Jesus. He is not talking about the difficulty faced because, for instance, construction of churches is not sanctioned (as in India) or prayer in public places is illegal (as in the USA). But he is talking of the reprisals faced when we decide to worship as a community or to pray where it is illegal.

For to complain about laws and refrain from doing what they prohibit is to concede that God has a superior somewhere on this earth. But to engage in what is prohibited is to proclaim that no place on this earth is beyond the jurisdiction of God. Moreover, if others do not like that proclamation, then we should be willing to face their wrath. What we do in the public spheres of our lives is an indicator of the extent to which we see God's kingdom operating. Are we willing to take this upon us? Are we willing to be God's ambassadors and face the wrath of others because of this?

Week 2, Day 4: Matthew 5.11-12

"Blessed are you when people revile you and persecute you and utter all kinds of evil against you falsely on my account. Rejoice and be glad, for your reward is great in heaven, for in the same way they persecuted the prophets who were before you."

During the past few years, many Christians have touted what they call "prophetic ministry" as the next new thing that the Holy Spirit is doing in the church. Charismatic leaders are said to "move in the prophetic." However, a close and hard look at what Jesus tells us about prophetic ministry reveals some interesting challenges to such thinking.

First, Jesus blesses those who will be persecuted and killed on his account because this reveals them to belong to the line of prophets. In other words, far from implying a grand and spectacular ministry, the phrase "prophetic ministry" should refer to ministry that results in the person being hated and harassed. A "prophetic ministry" should not be a glamorous one that draws thousands upon thousands to see one charismatic person perform. Rather, a "prophetic ministry" invites persecution.

But more importantly, we should expect this persecution to come from within the church! After all, it was the people of God who opposed the Old Testament prophets. The Old Testament is full of accounts in which the prophets are not accepted or persecuted by the people of God themselves. And Jesus draws a parallel between the prophets and those who are persecuted on his account.

Second, there is a rampant misunderstanding of what prophets were up to. Most often, we hear that prophets were in the business of giving words from God about the future. This is only part of the picture—and a small part at that. After all, few people are put to death because others disagree with what they say about the future. Rather, it was the present impact of a prophet that made him or her dangerous. The prophets called into question the practices of the Israelites and especially the king. They portrayed current events in theological terms and pronounced judgment upon the people of God for their failure to obey God and reflect God's character.

This was what was threatening. This was what made

others irate to the point that they were willing to kill the prophets. So also, we should find ourselves persecuted not when we predict the future but when we describe the present in ways that expose the darkness of present practices. More specifically, the prophets put their finger on systemic injustices rather than sins of individuals. So also, a disciple of Jesus is called to speak the truth to power by exposing systemic injustices that exist in our societies. Unfortunately, too many of us think that we need to point our finger at this or that sinful behavior that people may engage in. In this way, we subvert the role of the prophet and reject the true nature of our calling, which is to wage battle against the unseen principalities and powers - that is, the unjust structures - that oppress people. This will make the powers feel threatened, causing them to lash out against us through persecution.

This ties up well with what we saw in the previous devotion. Joining Jesus in his reconciliatory work, we bring down the wrath of others upon us. But that happens precisely because Jesus' work of reconciliation is the light that shines in the darkness to expose wrong ways of relating. While our work certainly has implications for the future, it happens in the present. Indeed, if it is not relevant in the present, we will work in vain. More importantly, if our work is readily accepted by all—or even by most—we need to question its validity and usefulness. If our discipleship is not threatening to anyone, especially any institution or power structure, we might be in need of re-evaluating it.

Week 2, Day 5: Matthew 5.13

"You are the salt of the earth, but if salt has lost its taste, how can its saltiness be restored? It is no longer good for anything but is thrown out and trampled under foot."

We concluded the devotions on the beatitudes in the previous devotion. We now move to the part of the Sermon on the Mount just following the beatitudes. In the beatitudes, Jesus had described the traits that define people who are transformed by the inbreaking kingdom of God. Now he moves to describe the purpose of such people in the world.

He does so with the use of a few metaphors. Commonly used in Christian circles, the metaphors have lost much of their original vitality much as a knife loses its sharp edge through use - and mostly misuse. It is imperative, therefore, to hone our understanding of these metaphors if we hope to understand what Jesus is saying in the next section of the Sermon on the Mount.

We are going to devote two days to this saying about salt and this is the first. Salt is essential to good health, but only in moderation. It has a number of functions. For centuries before refrigeration was invented, salt was used as a preservative. It was used to cauterize wounds. And it is still used as a seasoning to bring out the flavor of foods. Which of these does Jesus have in mind?

Probably the fact that the metaphor calls to mind so many common uses should leave us open to the possibility—indeed the necessity—that Jesus had multiple images in mind. We can certainly say that Jesus' disciples are in the world to preserve it from decaying even further. We can also affirm that the church is in the world as an agent of cleansing and healing. And, finally, we can say that the church is supposed to bring out the best in the world.

While this exploration can yield good insights, it is probably not where Jesus was going with the metaphor. Salt is useless by itself. Unless brought into contact with things that can "contaminate" it, salt remains inert. Eons would pass and it would remain the same—neither changing, nor producing change. It is only in contact with the clammy dampness of the world that the church can be itself. Hence, it is pointless—possibly counter-productive—to try to isolate ourselves from the world.

Furthermore, once salt has begun doing its work, the lines between it and what it is acting on becomes blurred. No one can un-salt food. We cannot remove the salt from the wound. And we could soak a piece of salted meat in water only to find that we cannot completely get rid of the salt. So, it must be with the church. Like the yeast that leavens the whole lump of dough, the church is to infiltrate the world, bringing the saltiness of the kingdom to every sphere.

Moreover, salt in large quantities is overkill. A little salt can pickle a large amount of food. A wound requires no more than a few grains. And recipes normally ask for a pinch of salt to taste. This should give us pause. The church is certainly in a battle. And the church will win the battle by permeating every aspect of life. However, the church will do so only as a minority! That is the paradox. The more salt one uses, the less it functions like salt.

So also, if the church becomes the majority in any culture, it will stop functioning like the church and become inert. We need only look at the post-Christian Western Europe in which Christianity is the state religion and in which the church is quite dead and the increasing Christian nationalism in the USA due to which the American church increasingly adopts more and more un-Christlike policies. Could it be that Jesus is warning us against trying to produce a "Christian society"? Could he be warning against optimism that the ills of the world will disappear if only everyone were Christian?

Week 2, Day 6: Matthew 5.13

"You are the salt of the earth, but if salt has lost its taste, how can its saltiness be restored? It is no longer good for anything but is thrown out and trampled under foot."

In the previous devotion we looked at Jesus' saying about salt. That was the first of two devotions on the saying and this is the second. In the previous devotion we considered some uses of salt and discovered that underlying all of them was the fact that salt functions only when mixed with what is not salt, and that it stops functioning appropriately in large quantities. We saw that the metaphor warns us against undue optimism—that is, the belief that we could cure the ills in our world if only everyone became Christian. Today let us consider another aspect of the metaphor.

Jesus rhetorically asks, "If salt has lost its saltiness, how can its saltiness be restored?" In Jesus' time salt, in Greek *halas*, was actually a combination of sodium chloride and gypsum. This mixture was produced by evaporation near seashores. Since sodium chloride is water-soluble and gypsum is not, high tides or rain would carry away the sodium chloride leaving mostly gypsum, which is not saline. In this way what Jesus calls salt lost its saltiness.

Now we have been nurtured so much on the 'once-saved-always-saved' doctrine that we often just ignore Jesus' words when he pronounces judgment on his disciples. Let us for once consider what he is saying. He entertains the possibility that salt can lose its saltiness, that salt can stop being salt.

From the metaphor, we are to conclude that Jesus is saying that a disciple can stop being a disciple, that a Christian can stop being a Christian—all based on the function or purpose of a Christian. In other words, a person becomes a Christian in order to do things that Christians do. If a Christian does not function as salt for the earth, the Christian will stop being a Christian.

What, then, of the 'assurance of salvation'? Here we must come to grips with a tension present in scripture. When God's people are suffering and things look bleak, God's word to them is a word of assurance and comfort. When God's people are living it up and become complacent, God's word to them is judgment and destruction. God's word is always directed where we are. It is situational and, therefore, personal. If we keep insisting on universals, we are asking a personal God to relate to us impersonally!

Frankly, very few of us are in situations of extreme suffering. Most of us are complacent. Therefore, we should take God's words of judgment more seriously than God's words of comfort. Jesus warns of having false security in a number of places in the Sermon on the Mount and we would do well to take heed. We need to honestly appraise our discipleship and see if we are becoming more like Jesus. If so, we need to press on. If not, Jesus is warning us that we may be cut off and destroyed!

I would make this assertion stronger. Unless we are actually in a situation in which we are being persecuted for our faith in Jesus, we must take more seriously the warnings about falling away. Pastors who constantly give their comfortable congregants messages of assurance are doing them a great disservice since God's word to those in comfort is always one of warning, not assurance.

Week 2, Day 7: Matthew 5.13-16

"You are the salt of the earth, but if salt has lost its taste, how can its saltiness be restored? It is no longer good for anything but is thrown out and trampled under foot. You are the light of the world. A city built on a hill cannot be hid. People do not light a lamp and put it under the bushel basket; rather, they put it on the lampstand, and it gives light to all in the house. In the same way, let your light shine before others, so that they may see your good works and give glory to your Father in heaven."

We have devoted the previous two days to Jesus' saying about his disciples being the salt of the earth. Before we proceed with the rest of the Sermon, I would like to spend this devotion on highlighting an important issue that arises from the difference between Greek and English.

A person accustomed to reading the bible in English is at a disadvantage because of a limitation of English. In the phrases "you are the salt of the earth" and "you are the light of the world," the second person pronouns "you" are plural. This is obscured in English. However, the predicates "salt" and "light" are singular. The juxtaposition of a plural subject with a singular predicate indicates that the subjects, though many, are to be thought of as a single entity. This is obscured in English because the second person singular and second person plural pronouns have the same form - 'you'.

We, therefore, easily commit an error that nullifies Jesus' intent—especially in these verses. We believe that Jesus is addressing an individual. Moreover, we believe he is speaking to us as we read the bible privately. This inevitably leads to private, individual interpretations of scripture. The result of understanding these verses as addressed to individuals is devastating and probably accounts for the ineffectiveness of the Church in much of the world.

That Jesus is addressing a group of disciples is critical. Moreover, that he employs plural rather than singular pronouns is telling. He is addressing the group *as a group* and not as a collection of isolated individuals. Just as no one would think of putting just one grain of salt to use, so also to think that one Christian can be the salt of the earth is ridiculous. Just as a beam of light cannot be broken down into its constitutive parts and still be light, so also one Christian cannot be the light of the world.

This is to say that Jesus expects his Church to be the agent of transformation in the world. However, the Church is to fulfill this function as the Church and not as a bunch of unconnected persons. This obviously speaks against the mudslinging that goes on between many denominations over issues such as spiritual gifts, baptism, communion, and worship.

More importantly, however, the notion of the Church as a communal force refutes the individualism rampant in much of the Church. In fact, frequently churches are structured in ways that promote individualism rather than communal life. Too often, church structures obstruct the ministry of the laity rather than promote it. Rather than expand our notion of ministry to include what God is doing in and through people, we try to force people into predetermined ideas of ministry. As a result, people often think that, to do what God is calling them to do, they must do it outside the context of the Church.

The outcome is that we have many people doing a lot of things without support from each other. It is no wonder then that the Church is seen as irrelevant and impotent in many parts of the world. If we are to be the salt of the earth and the light of the world, we need to recover the ministry of all believers in such a way that accords dignity to each person's contribution and affords each person the support of the entire Church.

Week 3

Week 3, Day 1: Matthew 5.14-16

"You are the light of the world. A city built on a hill cannot be hid. People do not light a lamp and put it under the bushel basket; rather, they put it on the lampstand, and it gives light to all in the house. In the same way, let your light shine before others, so that they may see your good works and give glory to your Father in heaven."

We have allocated two devotions to Jesus' saying about our being the salt of the earth and another one linking that saying to the one about our being the light of the world. In this devotion we will look at the second saying by itself. We will allocate two devotions to this second saying and this is the first of the two. So let us proceed and try to understand what Jesus meant in the second saying.

The metaphor of salt pointed to the *unseen* nature of salt when it is most active. The metaphor also included a warning, as we saw in the <u>second devotion on salt</u>.

The metaphor of light, however, carries no warning.

Moreover, it points to the *seen* nature of light. In this way, the two metaphors describe a tension that exists in being followers of Jesus. After hearing the metaphor of salt, we might be convinced that the people of God work best when they are hidden and innocuous. While that is true, it is also true that the people of God witness best when they are visible and dangerous. So, Jesus follows the metaphor of salt with the metaphor of light.

Now we are often so afraid that we might be calling attention to ourselves that we fail to take Jesus' words seriously. We point to Jesus' warning in Matthew 6.1. However, careful reading of both 5:14-15 and 6:1 should reveal that they are talking of different situations. In 6:1 Jesus is warning about doing things to gain approval of humans. Here, however, Jesus is commanding us to do good things so that others might have the opportunity to glorify God. In other words, there is the possibility that, if we do good things and remain silent, others may be led to glorify us! However, if we are clear that we do good things for and by the power of God, we make it clear that God alone is to be praised. And Jesus asks us to do precisely this.

We are to do good things in public, using each occasion

to point others to God as the source of the good that flows through us. To say that we are to do good deeds in public is to say that Jesus is not talking about private purity or holiness. In fact, Jesus is speaking of just the opposite. We have seen that the beatitudes are blessings, not on our individual piety, but on how we relate to others.

In line with this, we should expect Jesus to maintain the focus on the effects of our discipleship on our relationships. He is warning us against focusing on our personal impurities. What Jesus would have us do is focus on the impact our discipleship has on others. It is time we saw that emphasis. It is time we did away with the self-centered model of discipleship that seeks to make ourselves pure while disregarding the ways in which we treat people like dirt. Our light can only shine through the ways we act and behave. That is the only thing that most people get to observe about us.

This outward focus is quite different from the focus of common religions. The focus of religions tends to be on improving oneself. And hence, some of the most religious people are also some of the most self-centered people. However, discipleship to Jesus is different. We are expected to act and behave in ways that make others curious to know the

God we worship and the Lord we follow. The life of discipleship to Jesus is one in which the disciple shows off to others what this Jesus is like whom she follows. And by doing this, she allows her light to shine before others in obedience to Jesus.

"You are the light of the world. A city built on a hill cannot be hid. People do not light a lamp and put it under the bushel basket; rather, they put it on the lampstand, and it gives light to all in the house. In the same way, let your light shine before others, so that they may see your good works and give glory to your Father in heaven."

In this devotion we will look at Jesus' saying about our being the light of the world. Previously, we had allocated two devotions to the saying about our being the salt of the earth, a third devotion on the link between salt and light, and a fourth on the saying about our being the light of the world. This devotion is the second one about the second saying.

The metaphor of light is common in the Old Testament. Sometimes, it refers to deliverance (e.g. Jeremiah 13.16). It is used as a metaphor for good (Isaiah 5.20). At other times, it implies God's truth, wisdom, or instruction (Psalm 119.105). Isaiah applies it to the servant of Yahweh (42.6; 49.6), where the second passage clearly refers to Israel as a whole. Matthew characterizes Jesus' ministry as representative of

<u>Isaiah 42.1-9</u>.

So, by saying, "You are the light of the world," Jesus is saying something quite startling. His disciples are the means by which God had chosen to bring his light. Not only that! If we, as Jesus' disciples, insist that Isaiah 42:1-9 is about Jesus, then we have to also contend with the fact that Jesus applied v. 6 to us! In other words, being the light of the world is to be described by Isaiah 42:1-9. What would this look like?

For starters, Matthew <u>quotes</u> Isaiah 42.1-4 in the context of Jesus' healing ministry. Hence, being the light of the world can hardly mean less than being agents of healing in the world. But it is also to liberate along the lines of Isaiah 42.7— open the eyes of the blind, free captives from prison. So, when Jesus mentions "good works" in v. 16, he is not talking of being disciplined in our devotional time. Nor is he alluding to refraining from, say, gluttony.

What he is addressing is our joining him in his ministry of liberation. He is speaking of our willingness to speak out like the prophets, and like him, against the injustices of our day. And just as those who were so liberated by Jesus could not help but praise God for their deliverance, so also our "good works" will give rise to praise for God.

Jesus also tells his disciples that they are a city on a hill—a city that cannot be hidden. Whatever we do is visible. So, if, when we do "good works," people praise God, it follows that, if we do not do "good works," people will not praise God! If we find excuses for not imitating Jesus and for not becoming the kind of servants described in Isaiah 42.1-9, we will give those who are suffering, those who are ill, those who are prisoners of war, reason to question God's justice and love.

This calls for a radical allegiance to Jesus. Just as the prophets condemned the injustices of the monarchy and priesthood, so also, we should be discerning enough and courageous enough to indicate to the institutions around us—religious or secular, church or state—where they are going astray from God's character as revealed in Jesus. The question is, "Are we willing to take this charge, or will we find excuses for hiding?"

"Do not think that I have come to abolish the Law or the Prophets; I have come not to abolish but to fulfill. For truly I tell you, until heaven and earth pass away, not one letter, not one stroke of a letter, will pass from the law until all is accomplished."

The Sermon on the Mount began with a set of beatitudes in which Jesus described the traits of people who are transformed by the inbreaking kingdom of God. Then he moved on to a section in which he described his followers as salt of the earth and light of the world. We allocated five devotions to these two crucially important metaphors that speak of our role in the world.

Thus far, in the Sermon on the Mount, Jesus has not said anything that would warrant what he says in v. 17. This can only mean that the reason for his saying v. 17 lies further into the Sermon. In vv. 21-48, Jesus challenges prevalent interpretations of Torah, which could only have led to conclusions that he was dismantling it. To ward off such conclusions with the hope that his hearers would not prejudice their understanding of his purpose, Jesus prefaces the bulk of his teachings with this disclaimer. It is important that we realize this and take seriously what Jesus says about how Torah and his words relate to each other.

We might think that the disclaimer is unnecessary or even that Torah (the law) is obsolete. After all, are we not under grace rather than under law? However, it is precisely because we tend to think like this that Jesus' words are still relevant. In the second century, a Christian named Marcion declared that the Old Testament was irrelevant—indeed unfit—for Christians. His views were rejected by the Church. However, his kind of thinking lingers with us. We are quick both to affirm that the Old Testament is scripture and to declare that it is irrelevant.

We reject Marcion's position in theory while affirming it in practice. And because of this, we need to pay close attention to Jesus' words in this verse. Jesus clearly declares that the Old Testament stands as scripture to be heeded even in light of his work. His coming does not herald the end of the validity of the Old Testament. If anything, Jesus' coming affirms its validity. What Jesus does is to warn us against seeing too much discontinuity between Torah and his teachings and between the ministry of the prophets and his ministry.

Rather, he tells us that the significance of his teachings can only be understood when his teachings are taken to be fundamentally continuous with the Old Testament. When the church has forgotten or denied that Jesus' work is a continuation of the revelation in the Hebrew scriptures, we have engaged in many atrocities, leading to anti-Semitism of all sorts, with the Jewish people facing most persecution in supposedly Christian nations, and with these same supposedly Christian nations later pretending to make amends by supporting Zionism that deprives other people, in this case, the Palestinians, their land, their liberty, and their lives. We need to remember that Jesus is not a Christian. He was, is and always will be a Jew. He was a Jewish prophet. And his work is the final revelation in the sequence of revelation we find in our Hebrew scriptures.

This does not mean that Jesus does not challenge accepted understandings of the Old Testament. After all, if his ministry is much like the ministry of the prophets, challenging the status quo is exactly what we would expect him to do! In other words, his ministry should be seen as a critique from *within* Judaism rather than a rejection of Judaism. This is crucial and both Christians and Jews need to remember this. The *most* Jewish thing that Jesus did was call the Jewish people to repentance. When he announced judgment on the Jewish leadership and on the Jewish nation, this was just a continuation of what the prophets had done centuries earlier.

It is precisely because he did not abolish Torah that Jesus called the Jewish people to account in this great sermon. It is precisely because he saw its enduring relevance for the Jewish people that he declared that he had not come to abrogate it. But we also need to understand who he was speaking to. His audience consisted of Jewish people and to them he insisted that his words were not to be construed as abolishing Torah. But this *does not* mean that he would have said the same thing to Gentiles. Indeed, as Paul argues in Galatians, if we insist that Torah observance is necessary for Gentile believers, we fail to understand why God gave Torah to the Jewish people.

In other words, Jesus' claim that he was not going to abolish Torah does not mean that he intended non-Jewish people also to obey Torah. But just because Jesus did not intend for non-Jewish people to obey Torah does not mean that we should not study Torah and understand it and its role in the purposes of God for his good creation. Torah was and is a good thing. And it had a crucial role to play in God's plan to rescue his creation. But as we move forward in the Sermon on the Mount, Jesus will show us how we are to understand and interpret Torah according to the spirit that undergirds it rather than just the words used to express it.

Week 3, Day 4: Matthew 5.17

"Do not think that I have come to abolish the Law or the Prophets; I have come not to abolish but to fulfill."

The first thing we need to do in approaching Jesus' attitude to the law (or Torah) is to remember that Jesus lived in the first century and not in the times of the Reformation. This might seem a strange thing to say. However, most of us, who have had significant exposure to Protestantism, think along the lines of Martin Luther and other Reformers, who, in addressing the discipleship concerns of their day, focused on grace over against law. The lack of an emphasis on the grace of God in their times made them focus heavily on it. But this does not mean that Torah itself encouraged legalism or was given to promote legalism.

Indeed, in Jewish thought, Torah was a supreme sign of God's grace toward the Jewish people. Torah was God's gracious provision to the Jewish people containing the way of living that led to life. No matter how difficult it was to obey, it was not the burden we might consider it to have been. In the history of Israel, their deliverance from Egypt preceded the giving of the Torah. Grace always preceded the requirements of the Torah and hence Torah itself was the preeminent sign of God's grace to the people of Israel.

In line with this, Jesus says that he fully recognizes God's grace in Torah and that he will submit himself to it. We, who are colored by the Reformation concerns, might cringe at this. We contend that Jesus was saying that he would "complete" Torah, or "fulfill" Old Testament prophecy, or "fill out" the meaning of the Old Testament. However, the contrast with the notion of abolishing or repealing Torah requires that Jesus had its opposite in mind—namely, recognition of its continued validity, which could only be demonstrated by submission and obedience to it.

This does not imply that Jesus obeyed Torah mechanistically. God gave Israel Torah in the context of a relationship. It is not a dictator's demand on enslaved subjects. Rather, it is as much an expression of God's fidelity to Israel as the way by which Israel gave expression to its reciprocal fidelity to God. The underlying purpose was to delve ever deeper into that relationship with God in which Israel could ascertain God's character and will for them in concrete situations. Indeed, woodenly following the Torah might actually have been a sign of non-submission to it and we need to bear this in mind if we attempt to develop an ethic based on Torah.

And this is what Jesus sets out to do in the rest of the Sermon on the Mount, but especially Matthew 5.21-48. However, since he is going to at times come up against the generalized teaching of Torah to draw instruction for specific first century situations, others might conclude that he was subverting Torah or rendering it invalid. Jesus utters v. 17 to assure his audience that, notwithstanding the tension between his teachings and Torah, he was not circumventing Torah. His statement in v. 17, therefore, functions as a sort of disclaimer. Jesus is bringing to light a possible misinterpretation of what he was doing.

Hence, when we interpret Jesus' words in the remaining parts of the Sermon on the Mount, we should be careful. If our interpretation ends up making Jesus reject the Torah, then we have taken a wrong turn somewhere and need to go back to correct our understanding of the passage. This calls for humble submission to Jesus' words and a deep desire to be led by his Spirit. For unless we submit to the leading of the Spirit, we could quite easily end up making Jesus say something he never did.

Week 3, Day 5: Matthew 5.18

"For truly I tell you, until heaven and earth pass away, not one letter, not one stroke of a letter, will pass from the law until all is accomplished."

Here Jesus uses an oath formula "truly I tell you" or "in truth I tell you" to underscore his submission to Torah. Jesus is asking, "How can I undermine Torah when it has greater certainty of existing than heaven or earth?" To willfully disobey Torah while it was still active would be to call down on oneself the curse of Torah. What Jesus is saying, therefore, is that his teachings in the Sermon on the Mount are not subversions of Torah but validations of it.

Yet, at the same time, Jesus also pronounces the death sentence of Torah. When "all is accomplished" (NRSV) Torah will become inactive. The phrase "all is accomplished" is, however, quite vague and leaves one wondering what Jesus was talking about. Quite often, we link it with Old Testament prophecy and say that Torah will cease to be active when all the prophecies are fulfilled. Ostensibly, they are fulfilled by and in Jesus, meaning thereby that today Torah is invalid. Or others may propose that some prophecies will be fulfilled when Jesus returns, spelling the end of Torah's validity.

However, this would go against the flow and purpose of the Sermon on the Mount, which ends by depicting Jesus as the one who restates Torah for his audience and reaffirms that obedience is their sure foundation. So, what is Jesus talking about?

Probably the best clue is his reference to heaven and earth and their passing away. Jesus is affirming that Torah is valid here and now in the present creation. However, when the present heaven and earth give way to the new heaven and new earth, Torah will have become invalid.

So, Jesus is saying, "When God's purposes for this creation are accomplished, Torah will be rendered invalid." Torah, originally given to Israel as a sign and seal of their covenant with God, will no longer be necessary because the covenant will have been fulfilled. To be more specific, God *himself* will then dwell with his people, so Torah, the means by which God was present to Israel, would not be needed. At that time, God's people will not have to get instruction from Torah because God *himself* will instruct them.

However, in light of Matthew's use of the Emmanuel prophecy (Isaiah 7.14; Matthew 1.23) and Jesus' concluding promise, "I am with you always, to the very end of the age," (Matthew 28.20) we have a tension. If Jesus is present with us, then is Torah still valid? But, if Jesus is not fully present with us, can we say that Torah is invalid? Jesus' presence requires us to creatively apply Torah to our circumstances.

However, because his presence is not complete, we must apply Torah very carefully, being extremely careful not to jettison parts of it because of personal preference, nor, at the same time, blindly obeying out of fear or lethargy. This is an exciting prospect. It calls for active engagement with Torah in order to apply it to our lives. Too often we take the easy way out and just read letters off the pages of scripture, woodenly using the words of Torah *as is*, as though they applied to us in *that* form. This is a surefire path to legalism. On the other hand, some just read the text and say that this cannot be relevant for us anymore without bothering to wrestle with it. This is a surefire path to antinomianism.

The genuine path of discipleship is much more difficult. We are to take Jesus' hermeneutical method as demonstrated in the rest of the Sermon on the Mount and use those strategies to apply Torah to the various contexts within which we find ourselves. Jesus never had to deal with climate change or social media or free market economies. But we do. And so, we need to use his hermeneutical principles to help us navigate the new realities of our lives. How many will join Jesus in this task?

"Therefore, whoever breaks one of the least of these commandments and teaches others to do the same will be called least in the kingdom of heaven, but whoever does them and teaches them will be called great in the kingdom of heaven. For I tell you, unless your righteousness exceeds that of the scribes and Pharisees, you will never enter the kingdom of heaven."

Having stated his submission to Torah and its lasting validity, Jesus intensifies his commitment to it by moving to the issue of what would happen to a person who nullifies Torah and teaches others to follow suit. The sentence Jesus pronounces on teachers of disobedience is a complex one to understand. Two possible options stand out.

First, Jesus could be saying that false teachers will be excluded from the kingdom of heaven and that the citizens of the kingdom will think badly of them. This makes correct teaching concerning Torah a consideration in one's salvation! Such an idea is inimical to Torah. Indeed, contrary to popular assumptions, obeying Torah was *not* how Jewish people thought they would earn salvation. Rather, obedience was the response to God's already having brought salvation to them. So, to now say that a teacher could be excluded from the kingdom based on wrong teaching of Torah would make no sense within the teaching of Torah.

Second, Jesus could be saying that false teachers will indeed be included in the kingdom of heaven. However, they will be assigned low status because they led others astray. This runs against the widespread assumption that everyone in the kingdom will be equal. Such an idea, however, is nowhere in scripture. Rather, it has been imported into views of the afterlife from a romanticized notion of democracy, where "all men are created equal."

The point missed is that God's kingdom is precisely that—a kingdom. It is not a democracy. God will certainly respect us and deal with us graciously. He will love each of us immensely. He will deal with each of us equitably. But that does not mean he will deal with us equally!

Affected as we are by individualistic Western culture, we might find this position difficult to comprehend. Perhaps we can gain some understanding if we consider how it would be to attend a family reunion at which everyone knows that we had some secret struggle—say addiction to heroin—that became public since the last reunion. We would have lost face.

Losing face, however, would be beneficial in God's kingdom only if we rid ourselves of the quaint notion that we will be sitting on clouds playing harps and singing, and adhere to the notion that, like any kingdom, God's kingdom has levels of responsibilities. Those who have lost face will be given lesser responsibilities because they did not live up to the responsibilities they were given earlier.

I understand that this flies in the face of much that we have been taught. But please note that we are not talking about conditions for entry into the kingdom of God. This is not about salvation. Rather, it is about life in the kingdom of God. The Sermon on the Mount does not tell us how we are to enter the kingdom of God, that is, how we are rescued from the kingdom of darkness. Rather, it tells us what we can expect once we are in the kingdom of God. If we forget this and think that Jesus is describing the conditions for salvation, we will misunderstand him and the grace that God extends to us to rescue us.

But if we think that those who are rescued have no responsibilities, we will ignore Jesus' words, as has often been done, and make it seem as though God is unconcerned about how we behave toward others. To the contrary, since a kingdom can only function smoothly if the relationships between people are wholesome, God is deeply concerned about our behavior *right now*. And the Sermon on the Mount describes what behavior in God's kingdom would look like. But does this mean that, in the kingdom of God, there will be those who have actually lost face? What is Jesus really getting at in these two verses?

Week 3, Day 7: Matthew 5.19-20

"Therefore, whoever breaks one of the least of these commandments and teaches others to do the same will be called least in the kingdom of heaven, but whoever does them and teaches them will be called great in the kingdom of heaven. For I tell you, unless your righteousness exceeds that of the scribes and Pharisees, you will never enter the kingdom of heaven."

In the previous devotion we saw that a surface level reading of Jesus' words reveals two options: false teachers will either lose salvation or lose face. We saw that the Sermon on the Mount is not describing the conditions for entry into the kingdom of God. Rather, Jesus is describing what life in the kingdom of God looks like. At the end of that devotion I asked the question, "But does this mean that, in the kingdom of God, there will be those who have actually lost face?" So, what was Jesus doing in these two verses? What we need to do is approach Jesus' words in the way he approached Torah in the Sermon on the Mount.

If we treat Torah legalistically, we will find ways to

circumvent it and find loopholes. We will feel trapped by it and make it a burden too heavy to bear. This is what Jesus labels "the righteousness of the Pharisees." However, if we see in it glimpses of God's design and purpose, we can take Torah a step further. To do so would be to surpass the righteousness of the Pharisees. Jesus does this in the Sermon on the Mount. How do we use this approach to understand his words?

First, we must not believe that Jesus is laying down the law! Rather, just as Torah is primarily instruction rather than law, so also Jesus is instructing us. Second, we must allow Jesus the full use of language, including parabolic and hyperbolic language. Like a good rabbi, he asks us to choose between a rock and a hard place. This is not to confound us. Rather, it is to invite us to struggle with the instruction. Third, we should struggle with Jesus' instruction for only then will we make it our own. This means not coming away with a pat answer that might sound correct but which we cannot corroborate in our discipleship experience.

Rather, it means coming away scarred from the struggle, just as Jacob was scarred (Genesis 32.23-33), and, in like manner, emerging with a blessing.

So where do these three steps take us? Let me tell you where it takes me. The unsettling choices Jesus presents us should lead me to realize that what he is getting at is not a formula for who is in the kingdom and at what level. Rather, he is indicating the importance of the issue and that entrance into the kingdom of heaven is not as cut and dry as I might like it to be. Obeying Torah and teaching others to obey is extremely important. Indeed, I may not take it lightly.

Yet, no formula can assure me a place in the kingdom. Indeed, the rule of grace is precisely not the rule of law or formula. And Jesus is telling me not to take grace for granted. He is asking me to live in that gray area in which grace is still a miracle, in which discipleship is still an adventure, in which I grow even more dependent on him while understanding him better.

You see, the way to approach Jesus' cryptic words is to first believe that he knows what he is saying, that he *would not* ask us to do something we *could not* accomplish with his grace, and that he will give us the strength to obey him. If we think of his words as burdensome at any level, then it is *we* who have misunderstood him. For he himself says, "Come to me, all you who are weary and are carrying heavy burdens, and I will give you rest. Take my yoke upon you, and learn from me, for I am gentle and humble in heart, and you will find rest for your souls. For my yoke is easy, and my burden is light." (Matthew 11.28-30)

Life is complicated. And life in the kingdom of God even more so because we cannot use means that are in opposition to the purposes of the kingdom. Decisions are not going to be black and white in nature. And Jesus invites us to follow him in this difficult task of discipleship in the grays.

Week 4

Week 4, Day 1: Matthew 5.21-22

"You have heard that it was said to those of ancient times, 'You shall not murder,' and 'whoever murders shall be liable to judgment.' But I say to you that if you are angry with a brother or sister, you will be liable to judgment, and if you insult a brother or sister, you will be liable to the council, and if you say, 'You fool,' you will be liable to the hell[6] of fire."

So far Jesus has declared that he affirms the continued validity

---

[6] It is unfortunate that most of our translations continue to translate the Greek word *ge'enna* with the English word 'hell'. It is even more unfortunate that the lexical entries for *ge'enna* allow this *theological* interpretation to completely color the meaning of the word, rendering its origins in the Old Testament irrelevant. However, *ge'enna* simply meant 'valley of Hinnom', which is referred to in a number of places in the Old Testament. Likely a place where Canaanites and Jews offered their children as sacrifices to Molech, it later became a garbage dump that was kept lit so that the bodies thrown there would not have the chance to decay and putrefy.

It is clear that Jesus is using *ge'enna* as a metaphor for some kind of consequence. However, since he does not clarify the nature or duration of this punishment, any declaration of what *ge'enna* refers to is necessarily something that has been read into the text. However, in the Old Testament, it is clear that the link with Molech worship makes the main idea surrounding *ge'enna* that of a place of uncleanness and revulsion rather than of punishment and condemnation.

of the Torah. He was not abrogating it, but affirming it. And we will see that he does so in ways that would have shocked his audience just as it should, but unfortunately perhaps does not, shock us today.

We will see that Jesus upholds the Old Testament commandments while intensifying their demands. So, if we think that Torah was difficult and Jesus introduces us to some 'soft' and 'easy' form of 'grace', we will be unpleasantly surprised!

However, Jesus' goal here is not to place a heavier burden around our necks. That would go against the thrust of his teachings. What Jesus does is remind us that sin has a gestation period. It begins as something small and seemingly insignificant, which if nurtured will mature into full-fledged sin.

He directs our attention first to the sin of murder. Murder is merely the outcome of anger that is fed. Therefore, Jesus warns us in the most severe terms of the consequences of nurturing anger. He also tells us that anger expresses itself in our words. Therefore, if we find ourselves questioning the intelligence of another person or ridiculing someone's faith, we are allowing ourselves to nurture anger.

Here we observe that Jesus employs serious warnings on this issue of nurturing anger. Moreover, he leaves us no wiggle room. There are no exception clauses. Jesus does not allow ourselves the category of "holy anger." However, elsewhere in Matthew, Jesus becomes angry (21.12-17) and calls his opponents fools (23.17). The bible has other instances of God and humans becoming "justly" angry. How are we to resolve this tension?

The way forward is to realize that, while Jesus delineates different sentences—judgment, council, Gehenna of fire—for the three situations described—anger, calling someone 'raca', calling someone a fool—we are not to think of these as escalating punishments for increasingly severe infractions. Rather, Jesus is employing the full palette of language to provide an all-encompassing warning against anger.

Having done this, we need also to recognize that the bible is not a treatise of systematic theology. In other words, we do not have to iron out any tensions that may exist in scripture. Jesus' words here provide a sharp critique of passages in scripture that allow some kinds of anger. At the same time, the latter passages critique Jesus' words by pointing to examples both from Jesus' life and from the lives of others in which anger was the way of expressing God's desires.

On the one hand, we are not to use Jesus' words as a new law, in which he tells us literally the punishments due various forms of anger. When we see someone angry, we may not hurl these verses at them. On the other hand, we may not use the "permissive" scriptures to justify our anger. That kind of mutilation of scripture is precisely what Jesus critiques. Justification for anger must come from a conviction that justice—God's kind of justice—will not be served apart from a brief display of anger. And we may not assume that God's kind of justice comes naturally to us!

"So when you are offering your gift at the altar, if you remember that your brother or sister has something against you, leave your gift there before the altar and go; first be reconciled to your brother or sister, and then come and offer your gift."

In the previous devotion, we saw that Jesus addresses the issue of our being angry with someone. We saw that he warned against getting angry. In vv. 23-24, however, Jesus turns the tables for here our sister has something against us. In such cases, he tells us to take the initiative. We are to stop even the offering of a sacrifice for the sake of reconciling with our sister.

As in the preceding verses, Jesus does not provide us an escape condition. We are to pursue reconciliation not only when the wrong experienced by our sister is justified, but even if it is unjustified.

In other words, we are not to spend time and energy analyzing the possible causes of our sister's anger to determine if we have given her reason to hold a grudge. Such a pursuit is, in fact, merely an attempt to find a way—at times any way—of proving our innocence and of refusing to begin the process of reconciliation. Indeed, even if we do initiate the process of healing, we will make that a reason for thinking ourselves better than our sister. Jesus will not afford us such luxury!

Rather than devote resources to proving just cause for our sister's anger, we are to give our sister just cause for wanting the healing of our relationship. The difference between the two approaches is key. To try to ascertain if our sister's ill feelings are justified is to approach her with antagonism, as though she were a foe to be vanquished. On the other hand, to forego the issue of justification for our sister's anger and to make the first move toward the restoration of the relationship is to approach our sister with beneficence.

While Jesus tells us to be beneficent, we find that a bitter pill to swallow. We might acknowledge that Jesus would have us halt our sacrifice in order to attempt healing between our sister and us. However, we will quickly observe that Christians do not offer sacrifices anymore! Hence, does it not follow that Jesus' words here are not relevant to us?

How shrewd we can be! How slippery our arguments

are! However, they work only if we were to understand Jesus as requiring the halting of only sacrifices. That is not his intent. The sacrifice Jesus mentions here is probably the freewill offering that a person offers to show his or her love and adoration of God. It is an offering that displays the joy one has in God.

This is what Jesus asks us to stop in order to set things right between our sister and us. He is telling us that there can be no true joy if we allow our sister to hold a grudge against us. He is telling us that, in order to truly experience the joy of knowing God, we must first be reconciled to our sister. What Jesus is saying is that, if singing worship songs brings us joy, we are to stop singing; if preaching sermons makes us ecstatic, we are to halt the sermon; if reading uplifting books thrills us, we are to use a bookmark! All so that we can restore ourselves to our sister. In that, Jesus says, we will find joy in God.

Week 4, Day 3: Matthew 5.25-26

"Come to terms quickly with your accuser while you are on the way to court with him, or your accuser may hand you over to the judge and the judge to the guard, and you will be thrown into prison. Truly I tell you, you will never get out until you have paid the last penny."

In the previous devotion we saw that true joy comes from reconciliation. Jesus told us that, if there is any cause for estrangement within a relationship, we should attempt to make amends and build bridges. This is the source of true joy.

Now Jesus considers an example that his audience would have related to easily - and, in all likelihood, so do we. He presents his audience with another common occurrence: creditors, to force payment of unpaid loans, are hauling someone into court. Jesus, however, does not focus on whether or not the loan was ethical. He does not concentrate on the morality of usury or charging interest or if the interest rate was unjust or not. Rather, he addresses the aspect of the conflict. He portrays his audience as the debtor, who has the law against him or her. The law will insist that the debtor be punished and will imprison the debtor until payment is made.

What Jesus is referring to here is a debtor's prison, where people who defaulted on loans were imprisoned. There they would work to pay off their loan. However, given that a prison would not be engaged in producing products that were competitive in nature since that was not the prison's purpose, people would normally spend much longer in the debtor's prison paying off their debts than they would had they been free people. Despite this, what Jesus points us to is the inevitability of payment. There is no way to default on the loan for even imprisonment only serves to pay off the debt.

However, Jesus' emphasis is on the initial words "come to terms with your opponent in good time." Someone may hold a grudge against us. Jesus does not indicate whether the grudge is justified or not. Indeed, that is quite irrelevant. However, to ignore it is to allow it to foment in the person's mind, allowing it to grow in the person's mind and take on greater significance than it actually deserves. And there is no telling what the person will do to get even.

Moreover, once the person has crossed over to the point where revenge is necessary there is no way to talk him or her out of it for then even the smallest of offenses would have taken on the hue of an unforgivable sin.

The three situations in vv. 21-26 depict the progression from the offense—when we call our brother "fool"—to the nursing of the grudge by the brother, to the vengeance of the brother. We must first attempt to control our tongue. Having failed that, we should realize that there is a point of no return prior to which we need to be reconciled—be it when our brother quietly nurses the wound or when he actively seeks recompense for our indiscretion.

As always, Jesus places the onus of initiative on his followers—Christians. We are the agents of reconciliation, the makers of peace. So, the burden of setting things right falls on our shoulders. We are to be aware that there is a "good time" for making peace, a window of opportunity in which we can mend the relationship. We are to act within that window—not earlier for the person may not be ready to be reconciled, not later for the person may be past the point of reconciliation.

"You have heard that it was said, 'You shall not commit adultery.' But I say to you that everyone who looks at a woman with lust has already committed adultery with her in his heart."

As we continue with our series of devotions on the Sermon on the Mount, we move to deal with Matthew 5.27-28. In the previous devotion we saw the need for active reconciliation during the period when someone who has a grudge against us is in a frame of mind to reconcile with us. And we saw that we Christians, as Jesus' disciples, are supposed to be those who initiate reconciliation rather than wait for the other party.

Continuing his teaching on how to relate to others, Jesus quotes the prohibition on adultery from Exodus 20.14. Jesus does not soften the gravity of the act of adultery. Rather, he disabuses us of the notion that, as long as we do not 'go all the way', it is okay. He tells us that the lustful look is adulterous because to look at someone lustfully is to covet sexual relations with the person.

Surely this is too harsh! On the surface it may seem so. However, Jesus is not one to place an unbearable burden on us. He is here giving instruction on discipleship. How, then, can we correctly understand his words?

Consider this situation: I am walking down the road and I see someone who catches my eye. I gaze for an extended moment and realize that the person is quite attractive. I draw my eyes away, continuing along the road. Then come the dangerous moments.

What am I going to do with the attractive images so recently imprinted on my mind? Am I now going to recollect those images and mull over them ever so quickly in my mind? Am I going to think of specifics rather than generalities? Is the abstract notion that the person is attractive now going to transform into concrete images of how the person's hair and clothes looked and how those clothes accentuated the person's body? Then am I going to turn back for a second look?

The mind is very fast. Though reading the preceding paragraph might have taken tens of seconds, the mind can process it all in less than a second. That second look will begin before I have even blinked my eye! And it is all that leads to that second look that Jesus warns us about. It is the move from the general to the specific, from the vague to the concrete that Jesus warns us against. But if all the processing takes barely a second, how can we resist that second look?

Here we must remember that the mind can process wholesome thoughts as well as sinful ones. What we need to do is train our minds to consistently choose the fork in the road that leads to wholeness. At first, it will be difficult. When we do choose wrongly, we should recognize our folly, repent, and reflect on the process. In this way we will train ourselves to stretch that brief moment during which we process all the images of the first look. When the moment is stretched, we will find many marker points, such as described above, at which the process can be aborted.

And when we abort the process, make it a point to pray for the attractive person. Ask God to bless that person and draw him or her closer to Jesus. Ask God to provide him or her with health and security. Believe me, nothing stultifies the second look better than praying for the person. After all, if the second look dehumanizes the person, prayer "re-humanizes" the person!

"If your right eye causes you to sin, tear it out and throw it away; it is better for you to lose one of your members than for your whole body to be thrown into hell. And if your right hand causes you to sin, cut it off and throw it away; it is better for you to lose one of your members than for your whole body to go into hell."

As we continue with our series of devotions on the Sermon on the Mount, we move to deal with Matthew 5.29-30. In the previous devotion we saw how Jesus asks us to stretch the moments between the first look and the second look so that we have the ability to check ourselves before the second look begins and starts us down a path that leads to inappropriate desire and lust.

Now Jesus moves on to describe what measures we need to take to avoid the second look—and indeed any acts that are sinful. He is quite pointed and advocates drastic measures. If any part of us causes us to sin, we are to sever that part from our bodies. Do we take Jesus literally?

For instance, I could observe that I am prone to lustful thoughts, and castrate myself. However, this will not get rid of my lustful thoughts. The problem with sin is that much of it is indeed in the mind. Mutilating our bodies will not curb our wayward thoughts.

What then is Jesus getting at? He is using hyperbole to communicate a point—sin is serious business. In fact, so serious is it that Jesus even describes the possibility of our being thrown into *ge'enna* because we had failed to sever the offending parts of our body. While I don't think *ge'enna* refers to a place of never-ending torment and we certainly do not agree that our rescue depends on what we do, Jesus resorts to such severe language. Why? Why does he use such unsound doctrine?

Jesus is trying to teach his disciples how serious the issue is. It is so serious that resorting to exaggerations and hyperbole was necessary. Martin Luther, the German reformer, used to say, "I am saved by grace, not by works. Yet, not without works!" Perhaps that helps us understand what Jesus is talking about. As followers of Jesus, we need to have lives that reflect his teachings. We cannot say, "I am saved by grace" while habitually sinning. After all, God shows us grace in order to change us, not so we can continue to wallow in the filth of our sin.

So Jesus, through his hyperbole, poses us a question, "In order to follow me, are you willing to take the drastic measure of severing that part of your body that continues to drag you into the morass of sin?" It is similar to the angels asking Lot to flee from the comfort of Sodom, which camouflaged its corruption. "Are you willing?" is the question. If we answer, "No," we are valuing the sinful practice more than following Jesus. If we answer, "Yes," we are valuing following Jesus more. The way we show this, however, is not by going ahead and mutilating our bodies, but by shying away from the sinful practice.

Jesus mentions the eyes because that is the primary way in which we receive input from the world. And the hand is the primary way in which we act upon the world. We are neither to see nor to act in an evil manner. The evil eye and the evil hand are dangerous. We are to allow the eye and the hand no freedom to entertain evil. And, in the immediate context, the evil eye is the eye that entertains the second look we heard about in the previous session.

Week 4, Day 6: Matthew 5.31-32

"It was also said, 'Whoever divorces his wife, let him give her a certificate of divorce.' But I say to you that anyone who divorces his wife, except on the ground of sexual immorality, causes her to commit adultery, and whoever marries a divorced woman commits adultery."

Today we will deal with Matthew 5.31-32. From the issue of adultery Jesus moves to the related issue of divorce. In Jewish society, a husband could divorce his wife, but a wife could not divorce her husband. Some Rabbis permitted divorce on trivial grounds such as that the wife burnt a loaf of bread!

Jesus challenges this systemic abuse of women. They are not objects to be discarded at the husband's whim! Rather, the only reason for which Jesus allows divorce is adultery. He tells married men that they could divorce their wives only if she had committed adultery. Given the societal restrictions placed on women, this was certainly a rarity!

It is often observed that Jesus does not restore gender equality. After all, he does not say under what conditions a wife could divorce her husband! However, what Jesus has done is far more devastating to men. In vv. 27-28 Jesus has told us that we have committed adultery if we have entertained lustful thoughts about another person. Now, if a man wished to divorce his wife for the only reason Jesus permits—adultery—he would have to be certain he was not guilty of the same offense!

In a marvelous stroke Jesus restates God's original intention for marriage and protects it from abuse by men who would like to treat their wives as less than persons. Of course, it works the other way round too! Women may not treat their husbands as less than persons. However, in the context in which Jesus spoke, the more urgent teaching was that directed at men.

Jesus also tells us that, while we may be able to legally dissolve a marriage for reasons other than adultery, for such reasons the marriage remains intact in God's eyes! Hence, to marry someone divorced for reasons other than adultery is the same as having sex with someone else's spouse, which is adultery. Also, to marry someone divorced on grounds of adultery is to marry an adulterous person, which is adultery.

This teaching is hard these days when the divorce rate in the church is comparable to what it is outside the church. The solution taken by people is to water down what Jesus says, claiming that God's grace will cover the sin of divorce. While this is true, we should not presume on God's grace. A better solution would be to provide instruction on marriage to all young Christians much before they reach the point of seriously considering someone as their spouse.

But at the same time, we should also keep in mind that Jesus and Paul do hold out another option - that of being single. Both Jesus and Paul say that singleness is a valid and viable option for Christians. In a culture in which getting married was expected, both of them clearly say that there is no compulsion to get married. When we are addressing issues of relationships, sex, and marriage with teenagers and young adults, we should keep all of this in mind and not make them think that they need a spouse in order to become complete in God's eyes. In fact, both Jesus and Paul are clear that both marriage and singleness are gifts.

That such teaching is seriously lacking in the church is evident from the content of Christian materials directed at teens and young adults. This must change first so that people will marry with greater commitment resulting in fewer divorces or remain single without having an unhealthy idea that, till they get married, they are unfulfilled Christians. But for those who have married and who must unfortunately divorce after all these precautions are taken, God's grace will forgive, heal, and restore.

"Again, you have heard that it was said to those of ancient times, 'You shall not swear falsely, but carry out the vows you have made to the Lord.' But I say to you: Do not swear at all, either by heaven, for it is the throne of God, or by the earth, for it is his footstool, or by Jerusalem, for it is the city of the great King. And do not swear by your head, for you cannot make one hair white or black. Let your word be 'Yes, Yes' or 'No, No'; anything more than this comes from the evil one."

Jesus has been giving his disciples practical instruction for various situations in life. In this devotion we will deal with Matthew 5.33-37. These verses are related to the preceding ones. In both groups, Jesus advocates radical commitment in a world that lures us to find ways of remaining noncommittal or of breaking existing commitments. Whereas in the preceding verses Jesus tells us to remain committed to our spouse, in these verses he tells us to be committed to our words. Divorce and promise breaking are similar in nature because both involve refusing to live up to a commitment we have made.

The different oaths mentioned by Jesus—swearing by heaven, by the earth, by Jerusalem, or by one's head— might seem strange to us today. However, they were circumlocutions devised to create oaths that were not binding because they did not mention God. Jesus reveals the fallacy of such thinking by linking heaven, the earth, Jerusalem, and one's head (by way of God's providence) to God. In other words, Jesus says that oaths are binding despite all the sophistry we might employ to escape such a conclusion.

We misunderstand Jesus' purpose if we believe that he is prohibiting the taking of oaths, say in a court of law. Such thinking has led people to 'affirm' instead of 'swear' before secular officials. However, there is little, if any, practical difference between taking an oath and making an affirmation. Both are designed to insure that the person concerned speaks truthfully. So to insist that I will 'affirm' something, but not 'swear to' something is to play with words and to actually go against the spirit of what Jesus was trying to teach his disciples - and us through them.

It is to the issue of truthfulness that Jesus speaks. He is not saying, "Never take an oath" but "Always speak the truth." That is exactly what he means when he says, "Let your word be 'Yes, Yes' or 'No, No'" Jesus is telling us that we should be known as speakers of truth. When people hear us say something, their experience with us should lead them to know that we are speaking truthfully. They should have no reason to twist my arm—in this case by placing me under oath—to get the truth out.

A friend of mine used to insist on keeping his car windows open in the parking lot during worship despite the fact that a few cars had been broken into. When I asked him about this, he said, "Keeping the windows up would only keep the honest people honest." Taking this wisdom from my friend, we can observe that people who need to be placed under oath before they speak the truth are well able to commit perjury under oath.

Jesus asks us to be people who are so accustomed to speaking truth that oaths become perfunctory. We are not to take oaths to prove that we are telling the truth. Rather, we may take oaths since we would anyway tell the truth.

This understanding seems to run contrary to the surface reading of these verses. To be precise, it does! However, this interpretation is in accord with the spirit behind

Jesus' words. As mentioned earlier, Jesus refers to the various oaths then common only to reveal the error of thinking that there can be oaths that are not binding. His main intent in these verses is not to prohibit oaths but to correct an inadequate understanding of oaths and to engender truthfulness.

Week 5

Week 5, Day 1: Matthew 5.38-39

"You have heard that it was said, 'An eye for an eye and a tooth for a tooth.' But I say to you: Do not resist an evildoer. But if anyone strikes you on the right cheek, turn the other also."

In the previous verses, Jesus has spoken about how his followers are to behave. He has spoken about anger, lust, reconciliation, divorce and oaths. In all cases, he has placed a high standard before those who would want to follow him. But it is a standard that could result in others taking advantage of his followers. In the verses that follow, Jesus addresses these issues.

In Matthew 5:38-42, Jesus describes three concrete situations and suggests responses. We will dedicate a devotion to each of these situations. The first thing we should observe is that these three situations are oppressive ones in which his hearers play the role of the persons being oppressed. Jesus suggests responses that aim at allowing the powerless person to gain the upper hand non-violently through unexpected behavior. Jesus is describing ways of unmasking oppression, in which the oppressed person takes the logic of oppression to the extreme to unmask the oppression and reclaim his or her dignity.

It is important to understand the situational context Jesus paints and not blindly use the key phrase in Jesus' words out of context. Jesus' words are extremely precise and we dull their impact if we pull them out as though they were isolated words of wisdom like a proverb or koan. Rather, these words have power and purpose only when they are understood in their original context and we can make them relevant to us today only if we carefully understand what Jesus is doing through his words and then undertake the difficult task of translating his words to the contexts we face today.

The first situation Jesus describes is one that has been seriously misunderstood. So grave has been the misunderstanding that people have been asked to behave in exactly the opposite way Jesus envisions. Abused women, for instance, are told to 'turn the other cheek', thereby giving silent assent to the violence they experience. However, a careful analysis of Jesus' words reveals what he was getting at. And one principle we need to keep in mind while interpreting scripture is that the God we worship is opposed to oppression and injustice. Hence, any interpretation that underwrites oppression or injustice is to be treated with suspicion.

In that culture the left hand was not used in public. Only the right hand was used publicly. The only way someone could strike a facing person on the right cheek using the right hand was to render a backhanded slap. However, a backhanded slap was a way to degrade someone. For instance, the fine for punching an equal with the fist or hitting him with the palm was 4 shekels. The fine for slapping an equal with the back of the hand was 200 shekels! However, masters were allowed to slap their slaves and husbands were allowed to slap their wives and children with the back of the hand. This should give us an idea of what was considered socially acceptable behavior.

The backhanded slap, which required an exorbitant fine when between equals, was acceptable between people of unequal status. So what Jesus is telling the oppressed person is that he or she should respond to injustice in a manner that reclaims his or her dignity. The oppressed person should catch the oppressor off guard and paint him or her into a corner where he or she has no choice but to treat the oppressed person with dignity. Turning the other cheek forces the oppressor either to hit the person with the palm—that is, to treat the person as an equal—or to refrain from hitting.

Rather than ask his disciples to be doormats and just roll over in submission when they face injustice, Jesus was guiding his disciples to insist on being treated with dignity, but to do so in nonviolent ways that expose the injustice of the oppressor. Unless we understand this and keep it firmly at the front of our mind, we will misunderstand Jesus' words and, in all likelihood, use his words to oppress others.

Week 5, Day 2: Matthew 5.40

"And if anyone wants to sue you and take your shirt, give your coat as well."

We have reached a place in the sermon where Jesus tells his disciples how to navigate oppressive situations. In the previous devotion, we looked at Jesus' words about turning the other cheek and saw that Jesus was giving his disciples a way of challenging oppressive situations that recovered their dignity while forcing a change in the oppressor in nonviolent ways.

Continuing his description of ways of unmasking oppression, Jesus describes another situation quite commonly experienced by the poor in first century Palestine. According to Exodus 22.26, a garment taken in pledge had to be returned before sundown so that the poor person would not freeze in the night. However, this instruction was being obeyed so literally that the spirit of the words was ignored. Jesus paints a situation in which a poor person has borrowed money from a rich person and has given his or her only outer garment to secure the loan.

The poor person is unable to repay the loan and the rich person is trying to confiscate through legal procedure the inner garment because Exodus 22.26 placed restrictions on the outer garment and not on the inner garment. The rich were denying the spirit of the legislation by using silence as a loophole. I'm sure many of the viewers have heard of, if not directly experienced such oppressive situations in which those with money and power abuse the law of the land by resorting to some loophole that allows them to continue oppressing the poor and powerless.

Jesus suggests a course of action that is so outrageous that we often miss his point. He tells the poor person to strip naked and give the rich person his outer garment as well! If we take this to mean that Jesus is advocating public nudity, we will miss his point and find excuses for not obeying. However, if we consider the spirit of what he is trying to say, we will fare better. Through the act of stripping, the poor person is exposing the greed of the rich person. So concerned is the rich person about his money that he does not care if the poor person is warm at night.

By stripping, the poor person is saying that, given the opportunity, the rich person would even seek to possess the poor person's outer garment. And since the legal system was circumventing the spirit of Exodus 22.26 in favor of the rich person, the injustice of the legal system is exposed. It is a system that would unclothe people in order to make the rich richer! These days in which businesses and banks use their clout to trample on the common people and exploit them, we can truly understand how it is to live in an exploitative system, one that Jesus condemns.

Also, in Jewish culture when a person strips, shame comes upon the people who see him or her. This is seen in Genesis 9.20-27 where Canaan is shamed and cursed by Noah his father, Ham, saw Noah naked. By following Jesus' actions in the court of law, the poor person shames everyone who is present. The legal system is painted into a corner. They can either continue the injustice and face God's wrath for seeing someone stripped naked, or restore both garments to the poor person.

Unfortunately, these days businesses and banks have actually very little shame. They would not mind denuding a person in order to make a quick buck. And so as we continue to live in a system that helps the rich get richer, we should ask Jesus for fresh insights on how to challenge these oppressive systems in order to attempt to restore some modicum of dignity to the human race.

"And if anyone forces you to go one mile, go also the second mile. Give to the one who asks of you, and do not refuse anyone who wants to borrow from you."

We have reached a place in the sermon where Jesus tells his disciples how to navigate oppressive situations. In the previous devotion, we looked at Jesus' words about giving our cloak to the person who insists on taking our coat as a pledge. In the devotion before that, we looked at Jesus' words about turning the other cheek.

In both cases, we saw that Jesus was giving his disciples a way of challenging oppressive situations that recovered their dignity while forcing a change in the oppressor in nonviolent ways.

The third example of systemic injustice that Jesus addresses is from Roman law. Imperial law allowed legionaries to force natives of occupied territories to carry their load for one mile. However, in order to keep the conquered people from revolting, the law prohibited a soldier from forcing someone to carry his load for more than a mile. Soldiers who were caught ignoring this prohibition were severely punished.

It is here that Jesus comes in and says that, if a Roman soldier forces a person to carry his load, that person should insist on carrying the load beyond the first mile. The conquered person thus seizes the initiative. Imagine how humiliating it would be for a Roman soldier to beg to have his bag returned! He would be constantly looking around to see if his supervisor was around and had noticed that the native person was carrying the load beyond the first mile. In the presence of other conquered people, he would beg the person he forced to return the bag lest he face the severe sentence imposed on those who disobeyed the prohibition.

What has happened is that the conqueror has been conquered and the vanquished now calls the shots. No longer could a Roman soldier claim superiority over a Jew because he could force a Jew to carry his load. Certainly not after begging the Jew to return his property!

In these three examples Jesus reveals himself as an extremely creative person. And we should keep this in mind. Just as the three situations do not cover the gamut of human oppression, so also the instructions he gives do not provide solutions for all circumstances. He gives us models of creativity and invites us to join him in creatively disarming the oppressor through nonviolent means.

The primary goal is to recover the dignity of both the oppressed and the oppressor. Jesus aims at restoring proper relationships between the parties involved. By taking systemic injustice to the extreme, we reveal the system as unjust and leave the oppressor with no way to justify the injustice.

The final word in v. 42, of course, is subtly directed at the person who is in the position of taking advantage of another. The person has enough assets for someone to beg from him or her. Jesus tells such a person to be generous.

Having outlined creative solutions to three situations of oppression the implication is plain: if a person is in the position of taking advantage of another and acts on it, he or she will have to face such responses as outlined by Jesus—responses aimed at exalting the poor and humbling the rich! With such a warning, who would willingly choose to disobey Jesus? If Jesus' disciples would only follow his example in vv. 38-41, they would dissuade any would be oppressor.

It is important that we recognize that Jesus has not given us the full gamut of oppressive situations we can encounter. Rather, he has given us models in three situations. Today, we do not have the restriction on using the left hand in public, nor a marked difference in perception between a slap of the palm and a backhanded slap. Neither do we face a situation where we pledge our clothes to secure a loan. And soldiers today do not have the right to force the conquered people to do any labor. So in that way, Jesus' words in these three situations are quite irrelevant to us. However, the principle of overcoming oppression nonviolently is still very relevant.

What we need to do is use our imaginations in the oppressive situations we face. We need to prayerfully determine what nonviolent course of action would restore our dignity and the dignity of the one oppressing us. And we must aim at restoring the dignity even of the oppressor because he or she is also made to be God's image.

Week 5, Day 4: Matthew 5.43-45

"You have heard that it was said, 'You shall love your neighbor and hate your enemy. But I say to you: Love your enemies and pray for those who persecute you, so that you may be children of your Father in heaven, for he makes his sun rise on the evil and on the good and sends rain on the righteous and on the unrighteous."

We have just finished a section in which Jesus gives three concrete examples of nonviolent resistance to oppression. And we saw that Jesus invites us to resist human activities that aim to rob other humans of their dignity. While most people would, at least in theory, validate the idea of resisting oppression, such resistance has often been done in ways that Jesus might not have approved of.

Knowing this, Jesus moves to explicitly discussing how we should treat those who mistreat us. No other teacher ever told his or her disciples to love those who hurt them. It is contrary to everything we are led to believe and do. Enemies are enemies precisely because they have done something to earn our hatred. How, then, can we love them? This is how conventional wisdom goes. But Jesus does not afford us the luxury of adhering to it.

What he says is, "Look at it from another perspective. As my disciples, you ought not be antagonistic toward anyone. Hence, an enemy is not one who has hurt you, but one, who for some reason, is antagonistic toward you." It is the other person's attitude toward the Christian that makes him or her a friend or enemy, for the Christian ought have only one way of relating—in love.

What of those who persecute Christians? Have they not hurt us and become our enemies? Not so! People who persecute Christians do so because they perceive Christians to be a threat. And, in fact, Christians should be a threat to any oppressive status quo. By pledging allegiance to Jesus we become agents of deliverance and emancipation. Consequently, those who benefit from oppressive and enslaving situations will view us as enemies, become antagonistic toward us, and persecute us. In other words, becoming a Christian is not a neutral act. Rather, it is a declaration of war on oppression and those who stand to gain from injustice will view it as a declaration of war against them.

Jesus cites the example of God, who gives generously even to those who have made themselves his enemies. God does not consider them enemies. Rather, the wicked person acts wickedly because he or she has considered God an enemy. But God responds in love. And Jesus asks us to do the same.

However, we are quick to find any number of excuses to feed the enmity perceived by those who offend us. We speak of not becoming doormats. We urge Christians to be assertive. But this is not what Jesus instructs us to do. He tells us not to take the persecution personally.

People persecute us because they perceive Jesus incorrectly. He is the root cause for opposition toward us. We merely provide the opportunity for persecution. But it is our response that sets us apart. All others will retaliate. Many will do so violently. But Jesus' followers respond by praying for the offenders. We pray like Jesus, saying, "Father, forgive them for they do not know what they are doing." And indeed we can love and pray for those who hound us only if we truly believe that they act in ignorance of who Jesus is and of what he has accomplished for them.

But more than that, we are to love and pray for our

enemies because this is the generosity we see in our Father. Despite some (or is it many?) humans acting out of enmity toward God, he lavishes them with sunlight, and we can add refreshing breeze, fresh water, delectable fruits in trees, vegetables and roots from plants. He does not hold their enmity against them and use it as a reason to withhold his blessings from them. And we, his children, are to imitate the lavish generosity through our love and prayers for even those who hurt us.

"For if you love those who love you, what reward do you have? Do not even the tax collectors do the same? And if you greet only your brothers and sisters, what more are you doing than others? Do not even the gentiles do the same?"

In the previous devotion of the series, we saw how Jesus commands us to love our enemies. We saw that Jesus does not permit us the luxury of adhering to the conventional wisdom that we can hate those who have offended us. Rather, he asks us to extend our love even to those who have hurt us deeply.

Everything around us speaks against Jesus' vision of unfettered grace. We are taught never to become indebted to anyone lest that person gain a hold on us. Indeed, we often do people 'favors' only to remind them later of their indebtedness to us. In this way, we use even our 'good deeds' as swords of Damocles, and in so doing turn our 'good deeds' into evil. We could hardly remember a time when we did something for someone without expecting our kindness to be repaid. But, Jesus tells us that love is, at its source in God, unconditional.

Indeed to love someone is to set him or her free from any obligation to return our love.

That this is what Jesus is getting at is evident from his command to love our enemies. As we saw in the previous devotion, enemies are those who have an antagonistic stance toward us. Such people are hardly going to return our kindness. So Jesus tells us to love them. Since we can expect no kindness in return, such acts of love will be unconditional. What sets Jesus' followers apart is their willingness to love without strings attached.

Here it is important to note that we are not to love our enemies because they are enemies but despite their being enemies. That is, we do not find in their hatred toward us a reason for withholding our love. Rather, our love for them stems from God's love for them. Just as God loves them despite their enmity toward him, so also we are to love those who hate us.

Jesus is a master of human nature. We have already observed human reluctance to remain in anyone's debt. So, if we love our enemy, he or she might just be so uncomfortable at being at the receiving end of such generosity that he or she might in fact return our kindness. The person may not do it out of wholly wholesome motives. Nonetheless, our unmerited kindness could prompt a kind act in return. And if we make a practice of doing good in this manner, the other person might return our kindness so often that he or she forgets that we were 'the enemy'.

That is, of course, the best scenario. Most probably the person will either continue or even intensify his or her hatred toward us. Jesus tells us that in the face of even such unflinching opposition we should respond with love. This is what is distinct about Jesus' disciples. They respond to evil with good. In a world characterized by payback, by revenge, Jesus tells us to break the cycle of hate by positive acts of love. There is no denying that Jesus is asking us to do the exceptional.

Unfortunately, the church has often made the difficulty of Jesus' command an excuse for rendering his teaching void. We are told that the ethic of the Sermon on the Mount is so difficult to follow that its purpose is to make us recognize that we cannot do it without Jesus. Hence, the purpose of the Sermon on the Mount is to drive us into the arms of Jesus when we realize that we cannot follow Jesus' teachings here.

This is a denial of Jesus' teachings and his role as a teacher. As a teacher I know that I teach my students things that they may find difficult. However, the goal of a teacher is *always* to liberate the student and enable the student to live out the lesson as a part of the student's character. In other words, the difficulty of the teachings in the Sermon cannot be used as an excuse for not following Jesus' teachings.

Indeed, if Jesus is exceptional, can we expect him to settle for less from his disciples? Let us, therefore, be determined to do the exceptional thing of loving those who consider us their enemies. We are, after all, God's people because Jesus did that exceptional work for us!

Week 5, Day 6: Matthew 5.48

"Be perfect, therefore, as your heavenly Father is perfect."

In the previous devotion of the series, we saw how Jesus commands us to do the exceptional thing of loving people especially when we cannot expect anything in return. He tells us that unconditional love is what sets his disciples apart from other humans. Jesus is upping the ante with each verse it seems and now at the end of chapter 5 he tells us, "Be perfect, therefore, as your heavenly Father is perfect."

This verse smack dab in the middle of the Sermon on the Mount has proven to be one of the most burdensome verses in the entire bible. How in the world does Jesus expect us to be perfect? As Christians we are keenly aware of our frailty. We know that we live flawed lives. We sin by doing things we know we should not do as well as by not doing what we know we should do. Every day we struggle to be obedient to God. And, if we are honest, everyday we fall short of the life to which God has called us. How then can Jesus command us to be perfect? How can he have such a seemingly unrealistic command for us?

Two approaches have predominated Christian thought. First, some Christians have said that Jesus would not command us to do something that we could not do. Hence it would follow that we can be perfect. Christians who take this approach then try to define what perfection might be. They would draw a distinction between perfection and sinlessness. Perfection, they would claim, does not imply sinlessness for Jesus would not command us to be what we by nature are not. However, no matter how forcefully they insist that perfection is not sinlessness, they are never able to define perfection in specific terms except by reference to sins.

So John Wesley, in his essay, *Plain Account of Christian Perfection*, writes, "A Christian is so far perfect, as not to commit sin." The tremendous burden that this places on a Christian can well be imagined by those of us who struggle daily with sins. If I am already perfected to such an extent that I can completely avoid sin, then what do I make of the fact that I still do sin? And what does the word 'perfection' mean if it does not extend to include even my proclivity to sin? What kind of perfection is it that allows me to defile myself with sin, to abuse other humans through my thoughts and deeds, and to disobey the God I yearn to obey? This splitting of hairs approach that has no clear definition of 'perfection' only serves as a burden rather than something that liberates.

A second approach works from the fact of this struggle. Christians who take this approach have said that, since we continue to sin till we die, Jesus was not being literal. That is, Jesus was voicing a desire rather than issuing a command and Christians are to try to fulfill Jesus' desire though we will never entirely succeed. Jesus is saying, "I wish you could be perfect" or "Try to be perfect." This definitely is not burdensome for it takes into account the reality of the human situation. However, Greek had separate tenses for command and desire and the language in Matthew is quite definitely that of command.

The second approach is not honest with the language of Matthew. The first is not honest with the human situation. We are left to choose between a rock and a hard place. As a third solution, some Christians have tried to merge the two positions. The argument goes as follows: Jesus commands us to be perfect. However, we cannot be perfect. Hence, this is a hyperbolic command. That is, it is a command for an ideal world, not for the real one in which we live. However, this solution makes Jesus an incompetent teacher who gives irrelevant instruction and who concludes a class by undermining everything he has said so far.

The choices presented by these solutions are unacceptable for they force us either to be dishonest or to think of Jesus as incompetent. There must be a way out! What could it be? Not so fast! You will have to wait for the next devotion in the series for a hint at the answer.

Week 5, Day 7: Matthew 5.48

"Be perfect, therefore, as your heavenly Father is perfect."

At the end of the previous devotion in the series we were faced with having to choose between three approaches. The first two had elements of what I called 'dishonesty' and the third made Jesus look incompetent. The way forward is to do what the three approaches failed to do—namely look at the context to determine what the command might mean.

The preceding context deals with loving enemies and doing the exceptional as we have seen in earlier devotions. At the same time, the context is not very specific. Jesus cites God as the example of someone who loves his enemies and does what is not expected. However, the examples of sending rain and sunshine are not responses to specific acts of enmity. Rather, they exemplify God's general disposition. God is one who is inclined to bless those who oppose him.

We should take this as a clue to what Jesus is getting at. God's way of relating to his enemies by having the disposition of blessing them is to be the key to our behavior. This is the way of wholeness. Once we see that Jesus is not asking us to be perfectionists, we can take his command seriously. It is indeed possible to do good things for those who hate us. We may not do it all the time. But we may reach the point where we will not unthinkingly react with acts of hate.

Now, we should observe that Jesus turns love into something that is done. Jesus is not asking us to feel lovey-dovey about our enemies. He is not telling us to have affectionate thoughts about those who hate us. However, he is asking us to do good things for such people—probably despite our own feelings of animosity toward them! But the miracle is this: when we do these acts of kindness, it will erode away our hatred. We may never ever grow fond of people who hate us. But we may possibly reach a state in which hate no longer consumes us. And that is to be whole. Indeed, it is to be like God!

You see, Jesus is drawing heavily from the Old Testament in the Sermon on the Mount. For Matthew 5.48 in particular, he draws from Leviticus. You see, in <u>Leviticus 19.2</u> the Israelites first heard the words, "You shall be holy, for I Yahweh your God am holy." The command hinges on what the word 'holy' means. Similarly, in the Sermon on the Mount,

Jesus' command, "Be perfect as your heavenly Father is perfect" hinges on what the word 'perfect' means. Both commands are clear that we are to imitate God. However, the manner of imitation is quite unclear.

Over the years, the word 'holy' lost its original force designating something or someone as distinct or different. It came to mean something akin to 'pure' or 'sinless'. While these are true about God, they are not in the forefront when we call God holy. God is holy because he is wholly other, distinct from all other beings. His purity and sinlessness are merely a part of what makes him holy. Unfortunately, the focus on purity led to the misunderstanding of Jesus' command in perfectionist ways.

That Jesus is alluding to Leviticus 19:2 is most likely. And he uses a word not linked to issues of ritual purity precisely because the linking of 'holy' to issues of purity had rendered the word 'holy' burdensome. People strove to be pure and sinless without seeing these as merely ways of mimicking God's distinctness. Jesus, therefore, in a passage dealing with the distinctness of God, commands his followers to imitate that aspect of God's character. In this context, we mimic God by doing loving acts for even those who hurt us. It is certainly difficult. But it is not impossible.

We need to keep the active element of love in the foreground as Jesus does. As soon as we forget that Jesus is asking us to imitate God's actions we will stray. We will then try to imitate God's nature. And frankly, that is folly. We cannot be sinless and pure. Indeed, the more we try to be sinless and pure, the more we will sin and defile ourselves. The more time we spend on our purification, the more we will become impure.

However, if we spend our time acting in love toward our enemies, we will not have time to sin! That is the paradox of Jesus' way. The more I focus on myself, the greater will sin's hold on me be. But the more I focus on others—including and especially my enemies—the freer will I become. God, who is the epitome of freedom, is always other-focused. He creates in order to have an-other to relate to. He redeems in order to reconcile others who are estranged from him. In like manner, let us be more concerned about the wellbeing of others, thereby imitating God. And in so doing, let us find freedom.

Week 6

Week 6, Day 1: Matthew 6.1-4

"Beware of practicing your righteousness before others in order to be seen by them, for then you have no reward from your Father in heaven. So whenever you give alms, do not sound a trumpet before you, as the hypocrites do in the synagogues and in the streets, so that they may be praised by others. Truly I tell you, they have received their reward. But when you give alms, do not let your left hand know what your right hand is doing, so that your alms may be done in secret, and your Father who sees in secret will reward you."

In the previous two devotions in the series we dealt with Jesus' words, "Be perfect, as your Father in heaven is perfect." We saw that there are two aspects to look at. On the one hand, the perfection Jesus speaks of is a perfection that leads to wholeness in all our lives, especially in our relationships. On the other hand, the perfection he speaks of distinguishes us from those who are not his disciples.

In the whole section that precedes chapter 6, Jesus deals with relationships, not individual piety. And he has just finished instructing us about relationships in the kingdom. These are extremely important. However, because of their public nature, we can twist them. We can use people to parade ourselves as spiritually superior. We can act in order to receive praise. Our desire to be seen as doing good is so strong that we can subvert the very disciplines designed to deepen our relationship with God and others. So, Jesus now moves to issues of motive in relation to a few key Jewish spiritual disciplines.

The first discipline Jesus addresses is almsgiving. We should note that Jesus does not say, "*If* you give alms…" but "*when* you give alms…" In other words, he assumes his disciples will give alms. After all, if God is concerned about those in need, then he is concerned about those so destitute that they rely on alms. So Jesus is endorsing the practice while asking us to evaluate our motives. He tells us not to "sound a trumpet… as the hypocrites do." We are not to advertise our almsgiving in order to make people think that we are some kind of super-disciples. We are to give alms without fanfare and even without recognition.

But what does it mean to be a hypocrite? A hypocrite is a person who, in order to gain the approval of people, calls attention to his or her good actions. The things a hypocrite does are most likely good things, for people normally approve of good deeds rather than bad. However, the motivation for a hypocrite is the applause of others rather than benefiting someone else. A hypocrite is someone who is not critical enough about his or her own actions and intentions, always thinking that their motives are pure and their actions without any taint. Somehow, to trumpet our good deeds is to have tainted motives.

And it is here that Jesus asks us to check ourselves. We ought to do good deeds as an outworking of our imitation of God, who blesses everyone without thought of reward. We breathe the air God has generously given us without a thought of thankfulness. We drink the water he provides for us without an expression of gratitude. But he keeps giving. Hence, to seek commendation from others for good things we do is to deviate from imitating God. However, to give alms, for instance, anonymously is to bless as God blesses—incognito, silently, without recognition.

Jesus goes on to say that no deed is ever incognito. God

has his eye on us. He notices what we do and how we go about doing them. And he rewards those who bless as he blesses. Such people receive commendation from God because they have chosen not to elicit approval from humans. But here we must again check ourselves. It is easy to think that, if we are quiet about almsgiving, God will loudly proclaim to the entire world how great we are. To think that way is to deceive ourselves. Indeed, that is merely seeking human approval in a devious way. We need to remember, especially here when we try to imitate God, that God blesses incognito! For when God rewards us, we dare not think of the reward being any less veiled than our imitation of him.

"And whenever you pray, do not be like the hypocrites, for they love to stand and pray in the synagogues and at the street corners, so that they may be seen by others. Truly I tell you, they have received their reward. But whenever you pray, go into your room and shut the door and pray to your Father who is in secret, and your Father who sees in secret will reward you. When you are praying, do not heap up empty phrases as the gentiles do, for they think that they will be heard because of their many words. Do not be like them, for your Father knows what you need before you ask him."

In the previous devotion of the series we looked at Jesus' take on the discipline of almsgiving, one of the pillars of Jewish piety in the first century. We saw that he actually expects his followers to give alms, but that they should do so without fanfare and without drawing attention to themselves. In other words, the spiritual disciplines are not intended for others to think highly of us.

The second pillar of Jewish piety Jesus addresses is

prayer. Once again he tells us not to call attention to ourselves as hypocrites do. Here we need to remind ourselves that Jesus is not talking about corporate prayer. He is specifically targeting personal private prayer in this section. If it were corporate prayer it would make no sense for Jesus to tell his audience that they should go to an inner room and pray in secret. Corporate prayer just cannot be done in secret. But it is like his parable of the tax collector and the Pharisee, where both were giving utterance to private, personal prayer in a public setting.

What Jesus is saying in the Sermon on the Mount is that personal prayer is a relationship between God and an individual. Because of this, when I pray as an individual, I should place myself in a situation in which nothing intrudes on my relationship with God. Public places are dangerous because we are unlikely to be altogether honest. After all, we are not likely to air our dirty laundry in a busy street corner! Who would think of standing in church and saying, "Father, forgive me for I embezzled money from my place of work" or "God, have mercy because I had lustful thoughts about the person standing next to me"?

Such prayers are for private places because in private

we can be honest with God and allow him to forgive us and strengthen us to confess our sins to another Christian. Yes, I did say confess our sins to another Christian. While the sacrament of confession, practiced in some Christian traditions, has been abused, this does not mean that the practice itself is to be rejected. There is a genuine freedom that comes from confessing our sins to another person and hearing that person declare that we are forgiven. Of course, this needs to be done with care and with structures that safeguard the person who is making a confession and the person who is hearing the confession and pronouncing forgiveness.

Here also Jesus mentions the issue of reward. What reward, however, do we expect from prayer? If prayer is a relationship with God, then God will respond to our prayers to the extent to which we open up to him. If we parade our prayers in public and remain closed to God, we make the relationship dysfunctional. If we put on a façade of health, we will not allow God to act in our lives to heal and restore. Only those who are willing to cry, "Help!" will receive help. Those who are content with relating to God as though things were fine will receive the harsh reward of God's silence in their need.

While I have made it seem as though prayer were a

black and white issue, we who pray know it is not so. There is nothing we can do to guarantee that God will answer our prayers in the manner we desire. Prayer is not magic, working according to formulas. But prayer does require an attitude of transparency and submission before God. Jesus knows this. Hence, he urges us to go where we will not be tempted to be dishonest with God. Jesus tells us to go away from all the distractions of 'performance anxiety' so that we may bare ourselves to the only person strong enough and merciful enough to accept us no matter what we have done.

Week 6, Day 3: Matthew 6.9

"Pray, then, in this way: Our Father in heaven, may your name be revered as holy."

Here we will begin our exploration of the prayer 'template' that Jesus gave his disciples. The Lord's Prayer, as it is known, is prayed by millions of Christians every day and is, to a great extent, foundational to the Christian understanding of what prayer is and what prayer involves. Therefore, I will allocate six devotions to the prayer, this being the first one.

After warning us against pretense and repetition in prayer, Jesus gives us a model for prayer. The prayer begins by addressing God as Father. With the plural pronoun 'our' Jesus tells us to have a communal approach to prayer *even in* private. None of us has a special and unique claim to God for God is *our* Father. Yet God's people do, as a whole, have a special claim to God for he is our *Father.* The foundation of prayer, therefore, lies in the recognition of two crucial truths.

First, God is not some impersonal force or an emanation of the universe itself. Rather, God is personal and wishes to have a relationship with us. By referring to God as 'Father' we are reminding ourselves of this as we begin to pray. Just as a human father - at least the more conscientious ones - are favorably disposed toward their children and do whatever they can to benefit their children, so also we approach God with the declaration that he is our Father and, therefore, favorably disposed toward us and works for our benefit.

Second, God invites us into a family. Since we declare that God is *our* Father, we recognize that there are others in the family, our sisters and brothers in Jesus. Each of us is not brought into a family as only children but as one among many. There is no such thing as an 'individual Christian', for such a phrase is an oxymoron. Christians become Christians by being baptized into the body of Jesus, a community of mutual love and interdependence.

Jesus also tells us to remember that God is in heaven. This is not to be understood in a spatial sense. God is not 'up there' somewhere. Rather, as the third of these devotions on the Lord's Prayer will indicate, heaven is the place where God's will is done without opposition. God reigns in the heavens where his will is never opposed, never thwarted. This serves as a twofold reminder. First, we are reminded that there is a realm where, unlike the broken world in which we live, God's benevolent will is done without question. Second, we are reminded that the original heaven and earth reality that God created has been marred by human rebellion.

Attached to the address is the first request, "Hallowed be your name." This solemn request guards us against thinking of God as Father with presumption. We are called to remember that we are people who bear God's name in the world. Because we claim to worship Yahweh, the world will look to us for a portrait of Yahweh. That is, if we claim to be people who worship Yahweh, then the world will develop its understanding of Yahweh based on how we conduct ourselves. If we act in certain ways, people will conclude that we do this because of Yahweh's character. What we say and do reflects on the character of God.

Having prayed this first request, we may not act in ways that profane God's name without ourselves becoming hypocrites. Hence, to truly pray this request is to bind ourselves to doing only things that will indeed hallow God's name.

God's name here refers to God's reputation. This reputation is linked to God's irrevocable promises to his people and to the world. Having made promises, God is bound to fulfill them or risk losing his reputation. So to pray this request is to ask God to move history along toward the fulfillment of all his promises.

Of course, having prayed this request, we may not act in ways that obstruct the fulfillment of God's promises. For instance, we may not support oppressive practices that deprive people of food and clothing, for God has promised to bring us to a plenteous future. In the previous devotion, we saw that prayer is a relationship. In the context of a relationship, words become as swords, cutting both ways. We may pray for blessing but in doing so we commit ourselves to act in accordance with the blessing. We saw this in our devotion today.

To pray the first request of the Lord's Prayer is to commit ourselves to act in ways that hallow God's name rather than profane it. This responsibility accompanies prayer but God entrusts it only to *his* people.

Week 6, Day 4: Matthew 6.10

"May your kingdom come. May your will be done on earth as it is in heaven."

The second request in the Lord's Prayer is, "May your kingdom come." After his baptism and temptation, Jesus began his ministry with the proclamation, "The kingdom of God is near." In the person and work of Jesus, God's kingdom and reign had drawn near. Jesus had ushered in God's final reign. Of course, God's reign in its fullness is yet to come. That is why Jesus asks us to pray for it. It is commonplace in Christian circles to think that in this request we are asking God to come and reign in the hearts of individuals. However, such 'spiritualizing' of the request fails to take seriously Jesus' main thrust.

The reign of God, inaugurated by Jesus, is heading toward a consummation when God will set everything right. To pray "your kingdom come" is to plead for that day to be soon. It is to pray that this age will yield to the new age, in which God's reign reaches its purpose. However, as we saw in the previous devotion, prayer is a two edged sword. The issue here is whether we are indeed ready for God to grant this request. To pray "your kingdom come" raises the question, "Am I ready for that day?" The praying of this request should lead us to sincere soul-searching. If I am ready for that day, do I behave like it? Or does my behavior indicate that I am not ready?

Then there are the images that the word 'kingdom' brings to mind. For God's kingdom to fully arrive, other kingdoms will have to fall or submit. To pray "your kingdom come" is, therefore, an intensely political prayer for we are inviting a clash between kingdoms. By praying this request, we are questioning the oft-unquestioned sovereignty of all other political entities—including our own nations. Unfortunately, we have altogether ignored this aspect of prayer. We pray, not knowing for what we ask, and are then surprised when God's reign is not more apparent around us. For to restrict the kingdom of God just to the personal realm is to have a case of chronic spiritual myopia.

You see, the kingdom of God is not the idea of Jesus sitting on the throne of your heart. The scriptures do not have such a bland, insipid, and impotent idea of what the kingdom of God entails. As we have just seen, the kingdom of God is inherently political. After all, that is precisely what a kingdom is. If Jesus ruling my life does not impact how I behave toward others or does not affect what policies I support or does not alter my perceptions of how God is acting in the world, then I have an impoverished view of the kingdom of God and might actually be an agent who undermines the establishment of God's reign in the earth.

You see, many of us have accepted the idea that religious faith is a private aspect of a person's life between a person and God. This is a lie. After all, the supreme way in which God inaugurated his kingdom was through the death of Jesus - a public act intended to degrade and humiliate. On the other hand, others of us have understood that the kingdom of God has political ramifications and have attempted to enforce so-called 'kingdom values' on everyone. However, once again note that the kingdom was inaugurated by Jesus' death. The cross is both the ends and the means by which God brings his kingdom on the earth.

Now that we know, are we still willing to pray the request? When God's kingdom comes, it will call into question some of the policies that give us comfort. Economic and military policies that benefit us at the cost of others' lives and livelihoods will be judged and found to be sinful. When God's kingdom comes, we may have to give up the way of life we have been used to. When God's kingdom comes it will shake us out of our complacency. Are we ready for that? If not, perhaps we are safer not praying this request!

Week 6, Day 5: Matthew 6.10

"May your kingdom come. May your will be done on earth as it is in heaven."

The third request of the Lord's Prayer is "your will be done on earth as it is in heaven." This request is linked to the previous two requests in that God's will is to fully realize his reign in all of creation and so to hallow his name. Heaven, of course, is where God's will is always done. Earth, in contrast, is where God's will can be challenged and resisted. Heaven is where God's will is unopposed while earth is where humans and rebellious spiritual agents are able to oppose God's will.

Therefore, to pray "your will be done…" is to plead for the earth also to become like heaven—a place where God's will is not resisted. Of course, when earth becomes like heaven in this regard, history, as we know it, will cease to exist. In other words, to pray "your will be done" is to pray for the consummation of history, for the fulfillment of God's plans for his creation. But this does not mean that we just say the prayer and allow God to do what he wants. No! God wants us to be his partners in bringing about his will on the earth.

Hence, to pray "your will be done" is to accept one's role in bringing God's will on the earth.

We often think of this request in terms of determining what God's specific will for us is and then to do it. This is certainly within the scope of the request. Indeed, we ought to seek guidance from God concerning our lives. If God reveals his will, the request resembles Jesus' prayer at Gethsemane. He too prayed, "Your will be done." In light of his obedience in agony, we can say that this request is one of humble submission to the mysteries of the divine will. Indeed, to pray "your will be done" honestly, we need to be willing to accede to the divine will if revealed, no matter how absurd it may seem.

Yet, there is much more! As we have seen, this request covers God's overarching plans. We, therefore, must expand our understanding of this request to include God's plans. As it happens, it is easier to determine God's will in these larger areas than in the specific areas of our lives. It is easy to know that God desires forgiveness, love, peace, etc. Of course, obeying is not always easy. Most of us know that very well. However, no matter how difficult it is to obey God, once we pray "your will be done on earth," we commit ourselves at least to try to do God's will.

In general, we commit to try to forgive those who have offended us, to try to love our enemies, to try to be peacemakers, to try not to retaliate. It is better to try and to fail than not to try. However, too often we refuse to try because we know from experience that forgiving, loving, and making peace are difficult.

Yet, difficulty is never an excuse for not trying! In fact, as we have seen many times till now in the Sermon on the Mount, Jesus seems to have quite high expectations of those who follow him. We have two ways to take this. Either we say that he is placing an unrealistic standard in front of us so that, in desperation, we would run to him. This is not love. This is bullying, where someone in a position of power expects the unrealistic of the subordinate only to then appear 'gracious'.

On the other hand, we could believe that, along with the call to such high standards, Jesus gives us, through his Spirit, the ability to follow him. And even if we do not always manage to follow him, we know that we are enabled to do it some of the time. I prefer this approach. What about you?

Week 6, Day 6: Matthew 6.11

"Give us today our daily bread."

The second half of the Lord's Prayer begins with the petition "give us this day our daily bread." The Greek word *epiousios*, appears to have been coined by the Gospel writers to translate what Jesus actually said in Aramaic. The word is found only in Matthew 6.11; Luke 11.3; and in a second century Christian document known as the Didache. The meaning is uncertain and there is much speculation regarding it. A common thread in almost all understandings of the word is that it refers to something we need regularly, probably every day, in order to live. If we break it down into its constituent parts, a strategy recommended only when all others fail, it would mean 'what we need for our being', which gives credence to the idea that it might be 'daily bread'.

Of course, we can recognize that this common way of translating the request is symbolic. We are not asking God *only* for food, though that is certainly included. At the same time, we are not asking God only to provide for us daily. Rather, if we need something every minute, we are asking God to provide that thing every minute. So for the air we breathe, we might pray, "Give us clean air with every breath we take." Alternatively, for a home, when moving to another part of the world, we might pray, "Give us a comfortable home in the place to which we are moving."

In other words, the request is all encompassing. It is all encompassing precisely because our need for God is all encompassing. There is no area of our lives in which we can survive without God's provision. We need to keep this in mind when we pray, "Give us this day our daily bread." The notion of daily bread, however, is appropriate because of the ready link that can be drawn to the manna provided to the Israelites during their desert wanderings. Manna was to be gathered daily. Those who gathered more, in the hope of hoarding it, found that the leftovers had rotted during the night. This was God's way of getting the Israelites to depend on him daily. Their stockpiles could not provide for them.

In the same way, asking God for provisions daily can only be done faithfully if we are not in the business of hoarding provisions. This does not mean that we should not buy a big bag of, say, rice, which will last us a couple of months! It does mean, however, that whenever we dip a cup into that bag to cook for the day, we should do so with the attitude that we are dipping into God's provision. It also means that, if we are blessed with a surprise visitation of guests, we should be ready to dip a cup into the bag to provide a meal for them.

After all, if the bag is God's provision, we need to be open to the possibility that, on a given day, he intends to provide for others from it. To truly depend on God for our sustenance is to hold in open hands the gifts he gives us.

Some other interpreters have suggested that *epiousios* actually refers to the next day's provision. It is still daily bread in that it is still something we need every day. However, we are asking God to give us what we need a little before we need it. This enables us to be free from worry and frees us to focus on what is most important - loving God and our neighbors. As mentioned earlier, the exact meaning of *epiousios* is unclear. Hence, one should not be dogmatic about its meaning.

Whatever we conclude about the meaning of *epiousios*, we must understand that this request is intended to remind us of our complete dependence on God. We need his provision every day. Hence, when we pray this request, the first one focused on what we are to receive, we do well to recognize what we already have as a sign that God has granted this request in the past. I have enough today because God answered my prayer yesterday. And I had enough yesterday because he answered my prayer the day before.

Week 6, Day 7: Matthew 6.12

"And forgive us our debts, as we also have forgiven our debtors."

We continue with our devotions on the Lord's Prayer. After the petition for provision, Jesus teaches us to ask God, "Forgive us our debts, as even we have forgiven our debtors." Three points are worth noticing in this request. First, the Greek word *opheilēma*, just means 'debt'. 'Trespass' and 'sin' exclude too many things that Jesus includes in the petition. The petition encompasses debts of all sorts. We quite quickly think that the request involves sins. While this is true, there is more. Jesus wants us to think of debts in other areas as well—financial debts, relational debts, broken promises, rash and hasty words, etc. These are areas in which, for some reason or the other, we have failed other people, in which we have failed to treat people humanely or have taken advantage of them. Jesus wants us to keep these in mind as we bring this request before God.

Second, the second clause actually calls our attention to our past acts of forgiveness! Our forgiving ways are to be the reason for which we dare ask God to forgive us. We tell ourselves, "We have forgiven people. We have not acted in vengeful ways. We have released people from their indebtedness to us so they can live lives of freedom. We have set people free to obey God. We have not made it difficult for our debtors to follow God by holding them bound to us by our unforgiveness, which might, interestingly enough, not leave them with enough 'daily bread' for themselves and their families,"

With this knowledge, we pray this request with confidence that God will forgive us. Once we realize this, we can appreciate how serious this request is. If the assurance that our request will be granted is based on our forgiveness, then we need to become people who are quick to forgive.

Third, the small word 'even', often ignored by English translations, is powerful. We are challenging God to beat us at this forgiving game! We tell God, "Look at us. We are frail humans. We are prone to unforgiveness. Yet, even we have forgiven. Can the Author of forgiveness, then withhold forgiveness from us?" Like Abraham we challenge God and ask, "Will not the Judge of all the earth do right?" (Genesis 18.25). The assumption is that God, as the source of forgiveness, will see our forgiving ways and will not be able to contain the forgiveness within him. This is a gutsy request! Are we willing to spar with God in the arena of forgiveness?

Someone may, however, object that I have said that our request for forgiveness is based on our forgiving others. Such a person may think that I am promoting some sort of 'works righteousness' - the quintessential Protestant heresy. However, I have not added anything to Jesus' words. And most importantly, I have not removed anything! In fact, let me be very frank. If we need to twist Jesus' words in order to support some theological idea, then we need to junk that idea and cling to Jesus' words.

Jesus is clear in this request. "Forgive… as we have forgiven" is what he models for us to ask God. Jesus modeled this on the cross when he forgives those who had crucified him. Granted that he did not need forgiveness, his example tells us that there is no situation in which a Christian can legitimately remain unforgiving. If he could forgive those who had unjustly crucified him, then surely we can forgive anything that has happened to us.

This is the only request in the Lord's Prayer in which we ask God to mimic us! This is earth shattering because we normally expect to model ourselves after God. However, Jesus turns the tables here precisely so that we can see how crucially important forgiveness is in his kingdom. We are to become people who are so immersed in an ethos of radical forgiveness that we can dare ask God to look at us as models for him to imitate.

Week 7

Week 7, Day 1: Matthew 6.13

"And do not bring us to the time of trial, but rescue us from the evil one."[7]

Jesus ends the model prayer with the requests, "Lead us not into temptation, but deliver us from evil." Often we say these requests without noticing the strange paradox they contain. If God is to deliver us from evil, it follows that he has allowed us to be tempted. In other words, to pray "deliver us from evil" is to recognize that God will often not answer the prayer "lead us not into temptation."

This should not surprise us. We can recall Psalm 23 where the psalmist says that God leads him to green pastures and still waters. Why then does the psalmist talk about not fearing in the valley of death's shadow? The Lord's Prayer and

---

[7] The words "For yours is the kingdom, and the power, and the glory, forever and ever. Amen" are not found in the earliest manuscripts. Some or all of these words are found in various later manuscripts. It is unlikely that they were in the original since no scribe would have removed such doxological words.

the Psalm recognize an important part of authentic prayer. Prayer is a relationship. As in any relationship, in prayer God must be free to grant or deny our requests.

Therefore, when we pray "lead us not into temptation" we recognize that, at times, God will not grant that request. With that in mind, we add the request "deliver us from evil." What the two requests accomplish together is to ask for God's protection in all of life's circumstances. We ask for God's protection from and in difficult times.

What is the evil from which we ask God to deliver us? The second clause could read either "deliver us from evil" or "deliver us from the evil one." The ambiguity probably indicates that both meanings are intended. The second meaning is more straightforward since it refers to Satan, the evil one. The first meaning, however, is itself ambiguous. It could refer to evil that has its source outside us and of which we could be the victims. On the other hand, it could refer to the evil that has its source inside us and of which others could be the victims. The request is thus all encompassing. We ask God to protect us from all evil regardless of its source.

Very often some teachers teach us that the prayer of

faith obliges God to act. They then claim that, if our prayer is not answered, we must not have had adequate faith or appropriate faith. While this teaching seems to have infected many parts of the Church, it flies in the face of the last two requests of the Lord's Prayer. Jesus himself adds the 'but' before the last request, thereby preparing us for the times when the second last request is not granted. Hence, ironically, it may be true that at times the evil we need to be delivered from comes in the form of the insidious idea that we weren't kept from temptation because our prayers lacked faith! Jesus does not allow us to use prayer as a weapon to target any of his people. Prayer is the language of love between the believer and God and Jesus does not give a quarter to anyone who promotes the idea that one can control another believer by maligning his/her prayer life and/or his/her presumed lack of faith.

With this we have come to the end of the Lord's Prayer. What we have seen is that the prayer is simple, yet profound. This is probably why millions pray it daily and find that it still has remarkable potency twenty centuries after Jesus gave it to us. The prayer encompasses all of life, from our recognition of God as the one whose name we bear and whom we represent, to our understanding that this must reflect itself in how we forgive others, who will thereby get a taste of the forgiveness that God extends to all his beloved children. It encompasses a commitment to acting in ways that promote God's will and a request for protection against opposition that may come our way as a result of being agents of God's kingdom.

Week 7, Day 2: Matthew 6.14-15

"For if you forgive others their trespasses, your heavenly Father will also forgive you, but if you do not forgive others, neither will your Father forgive your trespasses."

Jesus adds a shocking addendum to the Lord's Prayer, in which he explains the request about forgiveness. This is the only request in the Lord's Prayer that Jesus felt he should comment on. It would seem, therefore, that he either considered the other requests absolutely clear and not in need of any explanation or considered this request to face some opposition from those who heard it.

In the addendum, Jesus inextricably links God's forgiving us to our forgiving others. A surface reading of these two verses could lead us to believe that God's forgiving us is contingent on our forgiving others. However, that would go against the whole thrust of the Sermon on the Mount, which portrays God as a lavish giver, who blesses both good and bad people without considering what their response will be. We need to keep this in mind, as we understand the two verses that follow the Lord's Prayer.

The way forward is to realize that forgiveness is a two-way street. On the one hand, the offended party must be willing to forgive. On the other hand, the offender must be willing to accept forgiveness, which requires an acceptance of guilt. In other words, every act of forgiveness is a 'drama' in which the persons play the part of either the offended or the offender. All of us have played both roles in the past. We have harmed others and we have been harmed by others. We have played the part of the offender and the part of the offended.

If we truly analyze the various situations, we will realize that we find it easier to blame others than to accept that we are to blame. After all, it is easier to say that someone else is wrong! And it is difficult to accept that we have violated others!

Jesus paints the picture of someone, who, having offended us, comes to us for forgiveness. This person has assumed the harder of the two roles by accepting to have been the one to blame. What are we going to do in this situation? If we assume the easier role and extend forgiveness, Jesus tells us that we will find it easier to come before God for forgiveness. Assuming the easier role makes the more difficult role easier to assume. If, on the other hand, we refuse to participate in the 'drama of forgiveness', by refusing to assume the easier role and to extend forgiveness, Jesus tells us that we will find it harder to come before God for forgiveness. Refusing the easier role makes the difficult role more difficult to assume.

In all situations, God is willing to forgive. However, are we willing to ask for forgiveness? The answer to this question lies in our willingness to forgive others.

As we saw two devotions back, forgiveness is a crucial part of Jesus' kingdom. There I suggested that the request asks God to mimic us. Here I have said that Jesus is asking us to accept the easier role of offering forgiveness than the more difficult role of accepting blame. When it is between us and God, we find it easy to accept that we are the ones who are to be blamed. However, when it comes to other humans, our pride often comes in the way of our accepting that we were the culprits in any given situation. However, as seen in both devotions, if we ask God to mimic us, then we are telling him to accept the easier role and forgive us when we admit to him that we are in his debt.

Week 7, Day 3: Matthew 6.16-18

"And whenever you fast, do not look somber, like the hypocrites, for they mark their faces to show others that they are fasting. Truly I tell you, they have received their reward. But when you fast, put oil on your head and wash your face, so that your fasting may be seen not by others but by your Father who is in secret, and your Father who sees in secret will reward you."

In the earlier parts of the Sermon on the Mount, Jesus has addressed two aspects of Jewish piety - almsgiving and prayer. Now he turns to a third practice.

The third practice of piety among Jews that Jesus addresses is fasting. There are often some misunderstandings about what this practice is supposed to be. First, it is not supposed to be an act whereby we deprive ourselves of good things. What would be the point of that? How is my not eating something I like a way of engaging in a spiritual discipline? Second, it is not supposed to be a means of telling God how serious we are about our faith. Fasting is between God and me. He knows my heart. He knows how serious my faith is. Hence, my fasting does not suddenly reveal to him the strength of my faith. Third, it is not supposed to be a way of earning God's favor—as though that could be earned! The very idea that the spiritual disciplines earn God's favor is abhorrent and should be discarded. What then is fasting supposed to be about?

The best way to approach Jesus' teaching is to keep in mind Deuteronomy 8.3, where we read, "Humans do not live on bread alone but on every word that comes from the mouth of the Lord." In this verse, we recognize that we have a dual sustenance. The presence of the word 'alone' indicates that humans *do* need physical food to survive. However, we also need to be sustained by God's creative speech.

Few of us live with a constant awareness that God is speaking to us. On the contrary, most of us live with our physical needs ever in sight. Most often, we are so overwhelmed with our physical needs that we overlook the sustenance that God's voice provides. Yet, have we ever seen someone walk around in shabby clothes and with unkempt hair claiming that he or she is doing so because he or she is abstaining from listening to God's voice? The very idea is ridiculous!

What Jesus does in these verses is tell us what fasting really is. It is a conscious act to abstain from one source of nourishment, namely food, in order to rely solely on another source of nourishment, namely God's voice. Therefore, Jesus tells us that our external appearance should not change since we should be aware of receiving the sustenance of God's voice even when fasting—especially when fasting!

Through these verses, Jesus asks us, "If not listening to God's voice does not lead you to an external show of deprivation, why should abstinence from food lead you to that? If you can display a 'not-deprived' face when you do not actively listen for God's voice, why should you act like beggars when you fast? Is God's voice not sustenance enough for you?"

The crucial issue that Jesus asks us to deal with is if we are ready to "taste and see that the Lord is good" (Psalm 34.8). If, while relying only on the sustenance of God's voice, we go about looking morose, we are saying that listening to God's voice is a chore we would rather do without. If that is true, we are better off not fasting!

Now, prayer and fasting are two disciplines that are

often seen as complementary. If, after much prayer, one does not receive clear direction from God, other Christians may advise a person to 'fast and pray'. Having read the devotions, the wisdom of such suggestions can clearly be seen. If we are asking God for direction, his voice is what we most need to hear. Moreover, to fast is to rely solely on God's voice. In other words, fasting puts us in the position of clearly hearing God's voice.

Of course, we should not treat the 'fast and pray' suggestion as a formula. While fasting, God may decide to speak to us about other things than the reasons for which we fasted. After all, prayer is a relationship in which God is free to grant or deny our requests. We need to keep this in mind when we 'fast and pray'.

We also need to keep in mind that forgiveness is the primary channel through which God works in our lives. If we are unforgiving people, we might become not only hard of heart, but hard of hearing as well! Unforgiveness might render us incapable of hearing God's voice even while fasting. Let us not sabotage our ability to hear God with our unforgiving ways. Let us be people quick to forgive, people receptive to God's word.

Week 7, Day 4: Matthew 6.19-21

"Do not store up for yourselves treasures on earth, where moth and rust consume and where thieves break in and steal, but store up for yourselves treasures in heaven, where neither moth nor rust consumes and where thieves do not break in and steal. For where your treasure is, there your heart will be also."

We are moving to an unnerving section of the Sermon on the Mount—unnerving precisely because it intersects our lives everyday. Jesus pits God and money as two contenders for our allegiance. Keep this in mind during the next few devotions and think also of the cheques you have signed, the credit cards you have used, the currency notes you have exchanged, the bank transfers you have made.

To people prone to hoarding things Jesus says, "Do not store up for yourselves treasures on earth." Almost without exception, we are pack rats. Therefore, Jesus' words are especially appropriate for us. We should observe that Jesus does not question the act of storing but the location of the storehouse. We cannot help but treasure things. However, to address the issue of locale, we need to ascertain what storehouses accomplish.

Storehouses serve a number of ends, three of which are relevant. First, they provide us with societal status. We are well aware of such measurements. People evaluate our worth by the car we drive, the house we live in, the clothes we wear, and even the people with whom we associate. These are our 'storehouses' of reputation.

Second, storehouses protect us from the vagaries of life. We are familiar with these too. We buy insurance of all sorts to guard against financial collapse. We build savings and retirement accounts to provide for us when we are no longer productive enough to earn a wage. These are our 'storehouses' to protect us against the effects of time.

Third, storehouses tell us where we have been in life. These are the people we have met, our photo albums, our home videos, and our portfolios. In short, our memories. They tell us from where we have come and give us a sense of where we are heading. These are our 'storehouses' of identity.

In light of this, Jesus asks us, "Who tells you your true worth? What gives you security in life? With whose help have you charted your life?" Simple questions. Annoyingly simple questions! We would almost rather he asked us, "Do you tithe?"! The questions are annoying because the answers are simple. To store up treasures in heaven is to look to God for our worth, for our security, for the plan for our life.

Unfortunately, this is probably the most difficult aspect of discipleship—difficult because we are daily faced with some new thing that promises to promote our worth—a higher paying job; to give us added security—investing in stocks for the future; or to be the path that is right for us—finding the perfect person to marry. None of these can satisfy because we know that "moth and rust [can] destroy, and… thieves [can] break in and steal" these things. There are jobs that pay more than my current job. The stock market can crash unexpectedly. The perfect person might leave us because he or she is too good for us. Or worse, we may be laid off, the country may go into a massive economic depression, or the perfect person may die. What do we do then? How do we recover our sense of worth, our sense of security, our sense of identity?

Jesus concludes the teaching about treasures with a valuable insight. We are devoted to those things or persons we trust for an evaluation of our worth, for security in life, and for guidance. Jesus tells us to place our trust for these issues in God, the only one who is permanent, and who constantly works for our benefit.

"The eye is the lamp of the body. So if your eye is healthy, your whole body will be full of light, but if your eye is unhealthy, your whole body will be full of darkness. If, then, the light in you is darkness, how great is the darkness!"

Without help from the context, we might think these verses are about 'seeing no evil'. However, these verses come in the middle of Jesus' teachings about 'treasure', 'money', and 'worry'. This should guide us. Further, in Jesus' day, the eye was considered not so much a receptor of information as a light that illuminated the world. What we might consider a metaphor would have struck Jesus' first hearers as a truism. The Greek word *haplous*, meaning 'single' or 'simple', was not normally associated with the eye. What then does Jesus mean when he says that we are to have a 'simple eye'?

Jesus is telling us to have a simple outlook on life, an outlook not complicated by the rat race of having to hoard provisions for the future. The simple outlook is consistent with Proverbs 22.9: "Persons with good eyes will be blessed, for they give of their bread to the poor." (Literal translation from Hebrew.) Just as Proverbs blesses the generous person, so also Jesus asks us to believe that God will bless those who are generous. The simple outlook looks at earthly treasures, recognizes that they are fleeting, and gives them away to benefit others while they last. The simple outlook does not try to hoard things that will rot in time.

Having just taught us about storing treasures in the right place, Jesus reveals the yardstick by which we can determine where our treasure is. If we have a simple outlook, our actions will show that we have truly considered earthly treasures temporary. If, however, we have an evil outlook, we will cling to our earthly treasures, showing thereby that we have stored treasures on earth.

Jesus then tells us what happens to a person who has an evil outlook. This person thinks that the resources in the world are in short supply and that he or she must accumulate as much as possible before someone else does so. This person then becomes so engrossed in the act of acquisition that acquisition becomes an end in itself. Rather than the original intent—not too noble of itself—of collecting in order to live, the person switches to a new intent of living in order to collect.

This is true darkness, says Jesus.

We recognize this darkness. We recognize it easily in others whom we call 'misers'. They are people who give with a closed fist. They are people who help with strings attached. We recognize them easily. Do we recognize them because to see them is to look in a mirror?

In these two verses, Jesus is asking us to appraise our perspective of the world. Is this a world of plenty or a world of deprivation? Is this a world created by a generous God out of the overflowing of his love or a world created by a ham-fisted god who gives only reluctantly? Our view of the world will play a huge factor in how we will live in it. Those who think that the world is rooted in stinginess will become stingy. Those who believe that the world is grounded in generosity will become generous. This is because we are creatures who cannot bear to live with dissonance in our lives. We desire to conform to the nature of things. Hence, in either case, whether we are generous or stingy, it will flow from our prior perception of the world.

This is why having an accurate idea of God's character and how he acts in the world is crucial. Theology, that is, thinking about God, is not some esoteric field that only professional theologians engage in. Rather, theology is done by everyone. It is what guides our actions because we want to live in accord with the world that God has created.

Week 7, Day 6: Matthew 6.24

"No one can serve two masters, for a slave will either hate the one and love the other or be devoted to the one and despise the other. You cannot serve God and wealth."

In the previous devotion, we saw that the 'good eye' belongs to a generous person, while the 'evil eye' belongs to a miser. Jesus now reveals the deities the generous person and miser serve. The generous person stores up treasures in heaven where God is. Therefore, the generous person serves God. On the other hand, the miser stores up treasures on earth. Therefore, the miser serves wealth.

Jesus pits God against money because that is how we function. We are taught that money is power. To have money is to have options and choices. To the contrary, the God Jesus reveals asks us to surrender power, and to give him complete allegiance. Money rarely becomes an end in itself. It most often serves as the means toward other ends—extravagant clothes, palatial homes, luxurious vacations, celebrity status, security for the future, etc. God, on the other hand, desires to be the goal of our lives. He will never be a means to other goals.

Therefore, we find it easier to worship money because money gives us some semblance of freedom, while God places his requirement of losing ourselves up front.

Jesus tells us that God and money have such diametrically opposed requirements that we cannot serve both at the same time. We cannot be generous hoarders or lavish misers! We know this. No wonder we try to justify our hoarding ways! We say, "I have to provide for my family" or "Jesus did not mean this literally" or "Jesus does not warn us against planning for the future" or "Jesus tells us to use money properly." There is some truth in all of these, which is why they are so persuasive.

Now, the Greek text has the word *mamônas*, an Aramaic word that means 'wealth' or 'money'. In this verse, *mamônas* and God are linked, signifying that *mamônas* should be taken as a personification, as the name of a false god. This is why earlier translations (KJV, NKJV, ASV) transliterated it with 'Mammon' while more recent translations render it as 'wealth' (NASB, NRSV) or 'money' (NIV, NLT, ESV, CSB, CEV).

It pays to observe that there never was a pagan god called 'Mammon'. Hence, Jesus is intentionally personifying 'money' as something that acts as a god even though we do not recognize that we are worshiping it. Recognizing Zeus or Krishna or Allah as gods that are not whom we should worship is quite easy. Any god who is named *as a god* is easy to avoid worshiping. However, it is the god that comes in surreptitiously, precisely because no one ever names it as a god that is particularly dangerous to us.

Indeed, by pitting money against God, Jesus does not merely depict money as evil. He casts the whole economic system, of which we are benefactors, in a bad light. Jesus labels as a false god the economic system that evaluates our worth based on our bank accounts, that promises us security in the future by impoverishing others in the present, that gives loans instead of gifts. This is the opposite of God's ways. Therefore, Jesus says that such an economic system is at the core idolatrous.

The false god of 'money' is so ubiquitous that we do not ever think that we are paying it obeisance. We have created systems in which it is impossible to function without 'money'. Hardly anyone would be willing to give me a meal or a room over my head in return for my labor. They will insist on paying me for my labor. And then I have to go looking for someone who will take this money and exchange it for food and shelter.

In other words, we have introduced money as a 'mediator'. While money has allowed for an easier process of exchange of services and facilitates travel, it is precisely because of this that we are unwilling and unable to extricate ourselves from its grasp. Now it no longer matters if I am able to work. Now someone must be willing to sign on a dotted line saying that they are willing to exchange money in return for my work. But once this happens, we become bound, like faithful devotees, to our place of worship - I mean work. Now, we will compromise because standing on principles might mean loss of livelihood, an impossibility before money became the god we all worship.

"Therefore I tell you, do not worry about your life, what you will eat or what you will drink, or about your body, what you will wear. Is not life more than food and the body more than clothing? Look at the birds of the air: they neither sow nor reap nor gather into barns, and yet your heavenly Father feeds them. Are you not of more value than they? And which of you by worrying can add a single hour to your span of life? And why do you worry about clothing? Consider the lilies of the field, how they grow; they neither toil nor spin, yet I tell you, even Solomon in all his glory was not clothed like one of these. But if God so clothes the grass of the field, which is alive today and tomorrow is thrown into the oven, will he not much more clothe you—you of little faith? Therefore do not worry, saying, 'What will we eat?' or 'What will we drink?' or 'What will we wear?' For it is the nations[8] who seek all these things, and indeed your heavenly Father knows that

---

[8] I have translated *ethnos* as 'nations' instead of 'gentiles' (KJV, NKJV, ESV, CSB) or 'pagans' (NIV) or 'unbelievers' (NLT). However, the primary meaning of *ethnos* is 'nation'. Given that the 'kingdom of God' is a 'nation', that is, a political entity, it seems clear to me that Jesus is contrasting the ethos of competing visions of what the ideal 'nation' would be.

you need all these things.”

I was tempted to break this passage down into individual chunks of one or two verses. However, they really function as a whole. Today we will look at the thrust of these eight verses. In the days ahead, we will look at some of the allusions to other passages of scripture to see what they tell us.

“Do not worry.” How easy it is for Jesus to say! However, is a worriless life possible? Jesus’ comparisons with birds and flowers do not help either! In Matthew 8.20 Jesus says, “Birds of the air have nests but the Son of Man has no place to rest his head.” In Matthew 10.29 he tells us about sparrows falling to the ground and being sold. And in Isaiah 40.6-7, the prophet emphasizes human weakness by drawing a comparison with flowers. All of these provide reasons for worry.

We must remember to whom these words were spoken. Jesus did not say these words to us. He said them to women and men who had already left everything to follow him. In the context of this relationship, Jesus tells his disciples not to worry. God knows their needs and he will provide for them.

The birds and the flowers become symbols of God's providence rather than models of quietude to be emulated.

Moreover, Jesus says these words to people he has taught to pray, "Give us this day our daily bread." We have seen how simple, yet all encompassing this request is. Having prayed this petition in faith, we can be assured that God will indeed give us what we need.

However, we know of Christians who pray, "Give us this day our daily bread" who go hungry and naked. Where is God's answer to their request? Ironically, the answer is given through others who similarly pray the Lord's Prayer. We—you and I—are the vehicles for God's answers. However, we know that to help answer someone else's need is to make our prayer for provisions all the more urgent. Most of us do not have unlimited resources. Many of us barely make ends meet. To provide for someone else might require that we reduce our standard of living.

What is our response to that? Will a simpler lifestyle alter the way we perceive ourselves? Will a more frugal existence make us more insecure? Will a lower standard of living result in a diminished sense of worth?

If we worry about food and clothing, what kind of food and clothing are we concerned about? Moreover, do we worry because we have diverted our resources elsewhere? That is, do we worry because we spend so much on luxuries that we push aside the essentials of life? How much of our concern is due to our relentless attempt to keep up with the Joneses?

With all these questions, we can see that Jesus is not really asking the impossible. Most of us have room enough in our lifestyles to pare down to the essentials. In so doing, we will also be able to act as vehicles of provision for those who have already hit rock bottom and who pray, "Give us this day our daily bread."

It pays to remember that Jesus is not calling individual people to live as isolated islands. Rather, he is calling individuals to join him in the formation of a community. This is the community in which worry is exorcized because the demons of self-centeredness have been silenced. This is the community in which the wellbeing of others is as important as our own wellbeing. This is the community in which each one looks out for the other. This is the community in which no one falls through the cracks.

Of course, we know that this is a far cry from *any* local church to which we may belong. Our churches are as broken as we are and very often forming a community characterized by mutual support is almost impossible. Yet, we have seen that Jesus never lowers the expectations he has from his disciples. If it is true that we cannot make Jesus' words a reality without a vibrant community where each one bears the load of the others, then the only honest way in which we can claim to be Jesus' disciples is to at least make the attempt to form such a community.

Week 8

Week 8, Day 1: Matthew 6.25-32

"Therefore I tell you, do not worry about your life, what you will eat or what you will drink, or about your body, what you will wear. Is not life more than food and the body more than clothing? Look at the birds of the air: they neither sow nor reap nor gather into barns, and yet your heavenly Father feeds them. Are you not of more value than they? And which of you by worrying can add a single hour to your span of life? And why do you worry about clothing? Consider the lilies of the field, how they grow; they neither toil nor spin, yet I tell you, even Solomon in all his glory was not clothed like one of these. But if God so clothes the grass of the field, which is alive today and tomorrow is thrown into the oven, will he not much more clothe you—you of little faith? Therefore do not worry, saying, 'What will we eat?' or 'What will we drink?' or 'What will we wear?' For it is the nations[9] who seek all

---

[9] I have translated *ethnos* as 'nations' instead of 'gentiles' (KJV, NKJV, ESV, CSB) or 'pagans' (NIV) or 'unbelievers' (NLT). However, the primary meaning of *ethnos* is 'nation'. Given that the 'kingdom of God' is a 'nation', that is, a political entity, it seems clear to me that Jesus is contrasting the ethos of competing visions of what the ideal 'nation' would be.

these things, and indeed your heavenly Father knows that you need all these things."

Yesterday, we looked at this passage as a whole. Today, I wish to focus on the implications of how we understand this command not to worry in light of Jesus' words in Matthew 8.20, where he says, "Birds of the air have nests but the Son of Man has no place to rest his head." The reason I am going beyond the Sermon on the Mount is because not worrying is a key element of the Sermon. We will never be able to become people who embody the beatitudes if we are always worrying about the future. We will never be able to be salt and light if we are distracted by worry. Hence, we have to weigh Jesus' words about not worrying in light of other things he says that actually could give us reason to worry.

When God tells us, "Do not be afraid" or when Jesus says, "Do not worry," they are really saying the same thing. But, if following Jesus means that we, like Jesus, might not have a place to rest our head, how can we avoid worrying? Here, when Jesus says that he, the Son of Man, is in a worse situation than birds, how are we to keep from worrying and being anxious? I mean, Jesus was single. It was relatively easy for him to live in 'perpetual motion'! What about those of us who have families? Many of us are spouses and parents. Can we completely stop worrying about our spouses or our children? Is Jesus just saying something for effect, something that is unattainable? Or is there something deeper to his words?

It is easy for us to dismiss Jesus' words by claiming he was saying something that is unattainable and that, therefore, must have been spoken for effect. But if we go down this route, we can dismiss *anything* he says about which we experience discomfort! Hence, I would not recommend such an approach. If it is true that, "No one has ever seen God. It is the only Son, himself God, who is close to the Father's heart, who has made him known" (John 1.18), then I must accept that, in Jesus, we have the definitive revelation of who God is and what his character is. Then the only option left to me is to wrestle with his discomfiting words and at least attempt to understand what he might have meant by them.

I must, therefore, conclude that it is possible, despite the unsettledness of discipleship, to live a life not characterized by worry. Indeed, Matthew uses the word *merimnaó* in the present active imperative form, which indicates an ongoing state of affairs. Jesus is not saying that we should never worry. Rather, he is saying that we should not have lives that are characterized by a continual state of worry.

Indeed, when we see Jesus, especially at Gethsemane, we understand that he was deeply troubled. In fact, in <u>Luke 22.44</u>, Luke writes, "In his anguish he prayed more earnestly, and his sweat became like great drops of blood falling down on the ground."[10] Here, the word translated as 'anguish' is *agónia*, which means "great fear, terror, of death; anxiety, agony." It seems that, according to Luke, Jesus was capable of experiencing "great fear, terror, of death; anxiety, agony." But he did this, at least from what we know from the Gospel, only while a Gethsemane. Yet, after a while, he was able to entrust his life into the hands of the Father.

----

[10] Verses 43 and 44 do not appear in some manuscripts. I refer you to the comment in *A Textual Commentary on the Greek New Testament*. I, however, am inclined precisely because the idea that "Jesus being overwhelmed with human weakness was incompatible with his sharing the divine omnipotence" would have motivated some early scribe to remove the verses to think that the verses were in the original. In fact, given that Justin, the earliest witness to these verses, lived in the 2nd century, many decades before $\mathfrak{P}^{69}$, seems to me to speak in favor of including these verses. In addition, there is scholarly debate about whether $\mathfrak{P}^{69}$ is from the Gospel of Luke or the highly edited version of the Gospel that was produced by Marcion.

In like manner, Jesus is not saying that we should *never* experience *any* worry. Rather, he is saying that, while we may experience worry and anxiety, there must come a moment after which we are able to entrust ourselves and the lives of those we love (after all, we worry most about them) into God's hands.

Week 8, Day 2: Matthew 6.25-32

"Therefore I tell you, do not worry about your life, what you will eat or what you will drink, or about your body, what you will wear. Is not life more than food and the body more than clothing? Look at the birds of the air: they neither sow nor reap nor gather into barns, and yet your heavenly Father feeds them. Are you not of more value than they? And which of you by worrying can add a single hour to your span of life? And why do you worry about clothing? Consider the lilies of the field, how they grow; they neither toil nor spin, yet I tell you, even Solomon in all his glory was not clothed like one of these. But if God so clothes the grass of the field, which is alive today and tomorrow is thrown into the oven, will he not much more clothe you—you of little faith? Therefore do not worry, saying, 'What will we eat?' or 'What will we drink?' or 'What will we wear?' For it is the nations[11] who seek all these things, and indeed your heavenly Father knows that

---

[11] I have translated *ethnos* as 'nations' instead of 'gentiles' (KJV, NKJV, ESV, CSB) or 'pagans' (NIV) or 'unbelievers' (NLT). However, the primary meaning of *ethnos* is 'nation'. Given that the 'kingdom of God' is a 'nation', that is, a political entity, it seems clear to me that Jesus is contrasting the ethos of competing visions of what the ideal 'nation' would be.

you need all these things.”

In today's devotion, I wish to focus on the implications of what Jesus says about not worrying in light of <u>Matthew 10.29</u>, where Jesus says, "Are not two sparrows sold for a penny? Yet not one of them will fall to the ground apart from your Father."

While songs like *<u>His Eye is on the Sparrow</u>*, written in 1905 by Civilla D. Martin, have taken this passage and concluded, "I sing because I'm happy, I sing because I'm free. His eye is on the sparrow and I know He watches me," I have never felt comforted by such lyrics.

You see, in Matthew 10.29, Jesus is clear that sparrows are sold and that they fall to the ground with the full knowledge of God. What security, then, do these words carry? What comfort can such words give us? When Jesus says that not even one sparrow falls to the ground apart from our Father, what image are we supposed to conjure in our minds?

Are we to think that God watches the sparrow in *powerlessness* or worse *indifference* as it falls to the ground, then probably making a note that there is one less sparrow available to fall to the ground? Are we to conclude, from the parallel drawn with our lives, that, when we die God watches in *powerlessness* or worse *indifference* as we breathe our last?

The problem with metaphors and visual images is that they are open to multiple interpretations. There are so many factors of the predicate that we can ascribe to the subject.

One example I have thought of before is Psalm 23. It is all well and good to compare God to a shepherd. However, the reality is that most sheep are eaten *by* the shepherd or sold *by* the shepherd! In fact, in the lyrics of the *Pink Floyd* song *Sheep*, this is just how the lyrics are taken. However, when David speaks of being taken to streams of water and green pastures, we understand that he intends to limit the metaphor of the shepherd to the provisions that the shepherd gives the sheep. Similarly, when he speaks of feasting at a table in the presence of his enemies, he intends to focus the metaphor on the protective role that the shepherd plays. In this way David enables us to interpret the metaphor of the shepherd along certain lines while excluding other lines.

In the same way, we need to see how Jesus was using the illustration of the sparrow. Jesus prefaces those words with,

"Do not fear those who kill the body but cannot kill the self;[12] rather, fear the one who can destroy both self and body in hell."[13] It is crucial to note that Jesus does not say, "Fear the one who *will* destroy," but "fear the one who *can* destroy." We are not to fear those who can inflict bodily harm on us but who cannot really damage our identities. God has the power to do that. He can destroy our identities along with our bodies.

However, just as the sparrow cannot fall *apart from* our Father, so also nothing can befall us *apart from* our Father. Jesus is pointing us to the fact that death is a reality in this broken world. He will not speak misleading words of comfort. Rather, by pointing us to the fact that the sparrow does fall to the

---

[12] I have translated *psyche* as 'self' instead of 'soul'.

[13] It is unfortunate that most of our translations continue to translate the Greek word *ge'enna* with the English word 'hell'. It is even more unfortunate that the lexical entries for *ge'enna* allow this *theological* interpretation to completely color the meaning of the word, rendering its origins in the Old Testament irrelevant. However, *ge'enna* simply meant 'valley of Hinnom', which is referred to in a number of places in the Old Testament. Likely a place where Canaanites and Jews offered their children as sacrifices to Molech, it later became a garbage dump that was kept lit so that the bodies thrown there would not have the chance to decay and putrefy.
It is clear that Jesus is using *ge'enna* as a metaphor for some kind of consequence. However, since he does not clarify the nature or duration of this punishment, any declaration of what *ge'enna* refers to is necessarily something that has been read into the text. However, in the Old Testament, it is clear that the link with Molech worship makes the main idea surrounding *ge'enna* that of a place of uncleanness and revulsion rather than of punishment and condemnation.

ground, he reminds us that we too are mortal. Just as the sparrow dies, so also we will eventually die.

However, when we die, it will never be *apart from* our Father. Even though he has the ability to utterly destroy us - body and identity - he will not do that. Rather, we are secure *even in death* in his hands. In other words, by placing the words about the sparrow falling to the ground *after* the word about God being the only one who *can* but who *will not* utterly destroy us, Jesus limits our interpretation of the illustration. We are secure and not *apart from* our Father *because* even a sparrow does not fall to the ground *apart from* our Father. The security of the sparrow, which is treated as a commodity and sold, is given as the basis for our security in the hands of our Father. We may have to go through all sorts of extremely difficult situations. But nothing can pull us *apart from* our Father.

While I have come to a different understanding of the illustration of the falling sparrow, I still do not resonate with the words of the song, because I may be able to sing, but I sing *despite* not being happy! I cannot deny what I am going through and act as though everything was well with me. To me, that itself would be a denial of the security I have in the Father, because it would seem that I need to reach a certain upbeat emotional state *before* I am able to confess that I am secure in him. Of course, that does not mean that someone else cannot find the song meaningful.

"Therefore I tell you, do not worry about your life, what you will eat or what you will drink, or about your body, what you will wear. Is not life more than food and the body more than clothing? Look at the birds of the air: they neither sow nor reap nor gather into barns, and yet your heavenly Father feeds them. Are you not of more value than they? And which of you by worrying can add a single hour to your span of life? And why do you worry about clothing? Consider the lilies of the field, how they grow; they neither toil nor spin, yet I tell you, even Solomon in all his glory was not clothed like one of these. But if God so clothes the grass of the field, which is alive today and tomorrow is thrown into the oven, will he not much more clothe you—you of little faith? Therefore do not worry, saying, 'What will we eat?' or 'What will we drink?' or 'What will we wear?' For it is the nations[14] who seek all these things, and indeed your heavenly Father knows that

---

[14] I have translated *ethnos* as 'nations' instead of 'gentiles' (KJV, NKJV, ESV, CSB) or 'pagans' (NIV) or 'unbelievers' (NLT). However, the primary meaning of *ethnos* is 'nation'. Given that the 'kingdom of God' is a 'nation', that is, a political entity, it seems clear to me that Jesus is contrasting the ethos of competing visions of what the ideal 'nation' would be.

you need all these things.”

<hr>

In today's devotion I wish to focus on Jesus' illustration about the 'lilies of the field', drawn from <u>Isaiah 40.6-7</u>, in light of his command about not worrying. The verses in Isaiah say, "A voice says, 'Cry out!' And I said, 'What shall I cry?' 'All flesh is grass; their constancy is like the flower of the field. The grass withers; the flower fades, when the breath of the LORD blows upon it; surely the people are grass.'"

With this allusion to Isaiah, Jesus reminds us that life is fleeting. None of us knows when we will draw our final breath. In this way, we are just like flowers in a field. The flower could be blown away by a strong wind. Or it could be scorched in the sunshine. And even if this does not happen, a flower blooms only for a few days. After that it withers and dies and is fit only as fuel for a fire.

In fact, Jesus switches from talking about 'lilies of the field' to talking about 'grass of the field'. This is striking. Hardly any of us would nonchalantly walk across a field of lilies in such a way as to damage the beautiful flowers. However, hardly anyone gives a second thought to walking across a lawn and stepping on the sturdy, yet not quite so beautiful, grass. "Consider the lilies," Jesus says to tell us about how God adorns nature with beauty that even Solomon could not equal. However, he switches to saying, "If God so clothes the grass of the field," while talking about the same thing. This is crucial to note because Jesus does not use any language to indicate that what he called 'lilies of the field' refers to anything different than what he later calls 'grass of the field'. The same thing is a 'lily' when it appears beautiful. But when it is no longer appealing, it becomes 'grass', fit for the consuming fire!

Isaiah too had this switch between 'flower' and 'grass'. If we do not find this switching between 'flower' and 'grass' in Isaiah and 'lilies' and 'grass' on Jesus' lips unsettling, we have not really allowed ourselves to be overwhelmed by the metaphor. The same person is treated like a 'lily' and as 'grass' depending on circumstances. If we have positions of influence or power, people will fawn over us. But if we have no influence or power, people will think nothing of trampling on us.

But Jesus is telling us all of this in the context of his admonishment not to worry! How are we to attain to such a state where, despite the changing fortunes of life, revealed in the differing ways in which people treat us, we do not worry?

I think, by pointing to God's provision for even the ephemeral flower, that is considered beautiful today but worthless grass tomorrow, Jesus is saying that God's provision comes *precisely* in the context of such rapid change. If our needs remained the same from day to day, any reasonably competent human could conjure up a plan that would ensure we are provided for. But it is in the face of life's rapidly changing fortunes that we need provision and sustenance. No human, no matter how competent, could ever live up to such a task. Only God can. Only God knows when I am flowerlike and fragile and so need to be handled with kids' gloves. And only God knows when I have matured enough for the gloves to be taken off.

In other words, what Jesus is saying is that the circumstances we find ourselves in, though most often completely unclear to us concerning why we are facing them, are ironically an indication of where God finds us in our lives with him. The more comfort we experience, the more we are still like flowers that need to be handled with extreme care. The more challenges we face, the more we have become like sturdy grass that can face even the consuming fires without losing integrity.

"Therefore I tell you, do not worry about your life, what you will eat or what you will drink, or about your body, what you will wear. Is not life more than food and the body more than clothing? Look at the birds of the air: they neither sow nor reap nor gather into barns, and yet your heavenly Father feeds them. Are you not of more value than they? And which of you by worrying can add a single hour to your span of life? And why do you worry about clothing? Consider the lilies of the field, how they grow; they neither toil nor spin, yet I tell you, even Solomon in all his glory was not clothed like one of these. But if God so clothes the grass of the field, which is alive today and tomorrow is thrown into the oven, will he not much more clothe you—you of little faith? Therefore do not worry, saying, 'What will we eat?' or 'What will we drink?' or 'What will we wear?' For it is the nations[15] who seek all these things, and indeed your heavenly Father knows that

---

[15] I have translated *ethnos* as 'nations' instead of 'gentiles' (KJV, NKJV, ESV, CSB) or 'pagans' (NIV) or 'unbelievers' (NLT). However, the primary meaning of *ethnos* is 'nation'. Given that the 'kingdom of God' is a 'nation', that is, a political entity, it seems clear to me that Jesus is contrasting the ethos of competing visions of what the ideal 'nation' would be.

you need all these things."

This will be our final pit stop at this passage. Today I wish to focus on Jesus' use of the word *ethnos*. Jesus says that the *ethnos* worry about what they are going to eat or drink or wear. These are not luxuries of life. Food and clothing are essentials. And Jesus says that we should not worry about these essentials because, in so doing, we would become like the *ethnos* rather than… Rather than what?

From the footnote, you will see that most translations use the word 'gentiles' or 'pagans' to render the word. Not only do I think these words are unhelpful since we rarely use such words anymore, but also I think that these words, even if correctly understood, miss the point Jesus is trying to make.

This is the first teaching segment in the Gospel according to Matthew. Following his baptism and temptation, Jesus goes to the Galilee region and begins proclaiming, "Repent, for the kingdom of heaven has come near." The reason behind his call for repentance is that the kingdom of heaven had come near. However, the word translated 'repent' is *metanoeó*, which means 'to change one's mind'. There is no religious or spiritual sense behind the word unless we bring it with us.

But why would Jesus call for a change of mind? His reason? The kingdom of heaven had come near! Somehow the proximity of the kingdom of heaven necessitated a change of mind. The kingdom of heaven refers to that realm in which God's will is done. It is the kingdom or political reality in which everything is set right, as we saw in the devotion on Matthew 6.10. When Jesus calls us to change our mind *because* the kingdom of heaven had come near, he is telling us that the great setting right had begun in and through his ministry. God was beginning to reign in the world.

What this means is that there was a new administrative reality that was invading the present reality. A new reality, in which everyone is provided for according to his/her needs, was making itself felt and known in the midst of the reality of deprivation that characterizes the administrative realities of the kingdoms of this world.

In other words, with Jesus' ministry, there was an administrative revolution taking place, one in which the dynamic needs of everyone (represented in the changing fortunes of the flower-grass) are taken care of. And what does one do when there is a revolution underway? One can either join the revolution or side with the entrenched system.

Those who refuse to change their minds have decided that there is only the reality of deprivation supported by the *ethnos* or nations of this world. But if we live in a reality of deprivation, we *must* worry because we know that no one is looking out for us and that the powers that be will strip us even of what we need if it would somehow benefit them.

However, if we believe that there is another reality to which we would rather belong, then we must join the revolution and live as though that reality were in effect today.

As an example, think of recycling. We are facing an uphill battle against our own proclivity for using non-biodegradable materials that harm our world. Some of us, however, recognize that the world cannot thrive if humans continue using such materials. And so some of us intentionally live as though these materials were unnecessary in our lives. Does this mean that the world has been saved from the deleterious effects of these materials? Absolutely not! Just because a tiny fraction of humans choose to live in a certain way does not mean that the problem is solved. However, such people show the rest of us that there is another way of living where we can thrive without causing harm to our world.

Jesus is calling us to do the same. He is asking us to recognize the inbreaking kingdom of heaven and partner with it by refusing to allow the *ethnos* or nations characterized by deprivation to define how we live. Yes, we may be stripped of everything one day. But the change of mind that Jesus calls for is the understanding that we can no longer say that no one is looking out for us because, with the arrival of his kingdom, God has taken on the responsibility of looking out for us.

Hence, Jesus concludes this section with the words, "Indeed your heavenly Father knows that you need all these things." This is not a guarantee that we will always have our needs satisfied, for we still live in a world where most people have not changed their minds about the deprivation that the *ethnos* or nations impose on us.

Rather, it is a sober reminder that, when two kingdoms clash - the nations of deprivation and the kingdom of God - there are bound to be casualties among the combatants. Those who align themselves with God's generous outlook may find that the nations of deprivation attack them precisely for taking such a stance.

However, just as even the sparrow cannot fall *apart from* the Father, so also no foot soldier of the kingdom of heaven will fall *apart from* the Father. The reason, then, for not worrying is not because everything will go the way we like it but because nothing can ever befall us *apart from* the one whose constant disposition toward us is one of love.

Week 8, Day 5: Matthew 6.33-34

"But seek first the kingdom of God and his justice,[16] and all these things will be given to you as well. So do not worry about tomorrow, for tomorrow will bring worries of its own. Today's trouble is enough for today."

Jesus concludes this section of the Sermon on the Mount with the words, "Seek first…" Of course, we immediately need to ask two questions. First, what does it mean to "seek first"? Second, what must we "seek first"?

Jesus' words address the second question more directly. We are to seek the kingdom of God and his justice. To seek the kingdom of God is to be on the alert for manifestations of God's reign. We know God's character. Therefore, when we witness events that reveal God's hand, we are to align ourselves with whatever God is doing. In this way,

---

[16] The Greek word *dikaiosune* is most often translated with 'righteousness'. However, *dikaiosune* also captures the idea of 'justice', which is the primary meaning of the Hebrew word *tzedakah*, which almost certainly was in the mind of the Jewish Jesus when he was speaking in Aramaic and in the mind of the Jewish Matthew, who chose to use *dikaiosune* to translate Jesus' words. Hence, I have chosen to translate *dikaiosune* with 'justice'.

we will be aligning ourselves with God's rule.

In particular, as we saw yesterday, this refers to our refusal to worry. Worrying is a sign that the nations of deprivation still rule the roost. But we participate in God's revolution and side with and work alongside his kingdom when we do not worry.

To seek God's justice is to desire to relate to others as God relates to them. Jesus is not talking about some nebulous concept of holiness that most of us understand in terms of purity. He is talking of specific ways of relating to others. God is wholly benevolent. God continually blesses those who hate him. God is a generous giver. So must we be.

What then does it mean to "seek first"? Jesus is not telling us that we are to first do something and, having done that, we can switch to doing other things. In other words, Jesus does not tell us that there are things we need to "seek second" or "seek third."

What Jesus means is that, above all else, we should seek God's kingdom. Our primary striving is to be for God's justice. We are not to strive for food and clothing. We are not to be obsessed with providing for ourselves. But we are to be obsessed with the kingdom of God and the justice that the coming of this kingdom entails for us and those around us. This does not mean that we should not plan for our next meal or buy a new pair of clothes. Rather, even these daily acts should be viewed through the lens of God's kingdom and as markers of his provision. For instance, splurging on a meal might not be in accord with God's kingdom when we consider that millions of people are starving. Buying an extravagant outfit might similarly be in discord with God's justice.

This might not sit well with you. It certainly does not sit well with me! However, no amount of maneuvering can get around the stark realization that, the more I try to justify my spending habits, the more I reveal that I serve mammon, the god whom all the nations of this world are enthralled by and enslaved to, and not the Father of Jesus, who desires that all should be fed, clothed, and sheltered.

The Jewish rabbi Hillel said, "The more possessions, the more care." However, it does not follow that "the fewer possessions, the fewer cares"! Indeed, people who are starving or naked do have intense care for their next meal or for something to wear and we dare not deny their legitimate concerns.

There is, however, a point at which the cares are at a minimum. At that point, we are content with what we have. Moreover, we are also able to give the largest proportion of what we have to those who have nothing. Jesus calls us to live at or around this medium of contentment.

Jesus does not even address people who have nothing. After all, they are the ones who truly pray, "Give us this day our daily bread" with urgency. Rather, Jesus addresses the human tendency of hoarding and increasing possessions. By addressing this tendency, he addresses most of us.

Jesus rebukes all our sophisticated thinking that allows us to accumulate more and more possessions. He tells us that accumulation is a sign of servitude to money. And no matter how much we attempt to escape this indictment of idolatry, we cannot. Indeed, the more sophistry we employ to escape the verdict of idolatry, the more we find ourselves bowing before mammon.

Week 8, Day 6: Matthew 7.1-2

"Do not judge so that you will not be judged. For by the standard you judge you will be judged, and the measure you use will be the measure you receive."

These verses comprise another section of largely misunderstood teachings. This is because Jesus employs a word loaded with meaning - 'judge'. He elaborates his teaching with two short parables. Unfortunately, these verses have normally been taken literally rather than parabolically. Let us allow these devotions to give us insight into Jesus' humorous and picturesque depictions of life.

The first part of Matthew 7.1 is probably the best known of all scripture. Unfortunately, it is as little understood as most of scripture. How often do we hear people say, "Don't judge me"? Even Christians do this, presumably because they have Jesus on their side. However, if we were to study Jesus' words in their context, we would find that he does not support licentiousness or a relaxed attitude to life. That is what we would expect from the person who also said Matthew 5.17-20.

Commands are easily misunderstood. Let us, therefore, address the most common misunderstanding of these verses. The English verb "to judge" has much the same ambiguity as the Greek verb *krinô*. The word *krinô*, has a wide range of meanings from 'separate' and 'distinguish' to 'judge' and 'think' to 'condemn' and 'sentence'. Therefore, the context must determine the meaning. Since, in the rest of the Sermon, Jesus advocates discernment, but proscribes condemning, *krinô* cannot mean 'discern' or 'correct' in Matthew 7.1-2.

That is not all! The two verses we are addressing make no sense if Jesus is saying, "Do not correct." For then he would be saying, "Do not correct, so that you may not be corrected." That Jesus is not so shallow a teacher should be evident to anyone who has seriously read the preceding sections of the Sermon on the Mount, especially the concluding part of chapter 6 where Jesus charges us not to worry. Jesus would never issue such an asinine command about not being discerning or making judgments, for not only does it fail to motivate us not to correct others, but also it tries to motivate us at the most contemptible level possible. However, if anything, people have found the Sermon on the Mount difficult to obey rather than easy. Rather than provide us ways of being shoddy disciples, in the Sermon Jesus charts the high-ground of discipleship that he would have us trod.

Of course, to say that we are to exercise discernment does not imply that we are to function as "holy policemen"! In the next devotion we will see exactly what it is that Jesus prohibits. Moreover, in the three devotions after that, we will see how Jesus would have us exercise discernment.

However, for today it is best we understand that, since we find it quite easy to condemn people and sentence them, this is most surely exactly what Jesus was proscribing. In other words, knowing that Jesus' words are most often quite difficult to obey, any interpretation that aligns too well with our natural inclination is probably not going to be aligned with what Jesus means when he teaches us.

Week 8, Day 7: Matthew 7.1-2

"Do not judge so that you will not be judged. For by the standard you judge you will be judged, and the measure you use will be the measure you receive."

In the previous devotion, we addressed one of the most common misunderstandings of v. 1. We considered a prime example of what Jesus is not saying in these verses. Today let us address the issue of what Jesus did mean.

In the first part of Matthew 7, Jesus tells us how to deal with others, especially when we observe that their behavior and ours are different. In the previous devotion, we saw that Jesus actually endorses discernment. We are first to determine if the difference is essential. If we decide that it is, we are to correct the other person. Jesus' words address the matter of how we go about doing this.

Correcting others is tricky business, which is why Jesus even tackles the issue. Jesus warns us in no uncertain terms that, in correcting another Christian, we must not call into question the person's salvation. This is what would happen if we take *krinō* to mean 'condemn'. Now, this is not all that difficult. Few of us readily jump from telling another Christian, "You are sinning" to saying, "You will end up in hell." I mean, I hope most of us are not quick to make such a leap!

However, Jesus' words touch on a more subtle aspect of correction. He tells us that we should not assign consequences for the person's behavior. This is difficult—almost impossible—for most of us, especially today when the cause-and-effect worldview of science reigns supreme. How easily we tell a smoker that she will have lung cancer, or an alcoholic that his liver will stop functioning! How unthinkingly we tell a person who diets on fast-food that he will suffer cardiac arrest or someone who does not exercise that she has a short life expectancy! And what about moral issues? Do we not tell an embezzler that she will end up in jail or an adulterer that his wife will divorce him?

All these responses constitute condemning a person. Jesus warns us against this kind of condemning for two reasons. First, following Jesus may be difficult, but it is not meant to be done out of fear. Jesus is, after all, the one who speaks the divine "do not be afraid." We are to follow Jesus not because not doing so would land us in hell, but because

Jesus is worth following. This is a crucial point. Too often we use the 'heaven and hell' trope as a kind of carrot and stick approach with people. Most of our evangelistic strategies are nothing short of scaremongering, with the threat of hellfires intended to make people run to Jesus. Quite frankly, if Jesus needs a hell for anyone to become his disciple, I would rather not be his disciple!

Second, the kind of condemning I mentioned above excludes grace. However, grace is that marvelous miracle by which God rescues us from the tyranny of cause-and-effect. And in a world infused with God's grace, we may no longer say, "You have done such and such, therefore, you will reap such and such." Grace is the liberation from any idea that there has to be a payment for things that are done. Grace is the ultimate Christian anti-*karmic* doctrine and we dare not forget it.

This is why Jesus tells us not to pass judgment on anyone as though we had been appointed judge over anyone. Since, in his kingdom, the 'rule of law' is replaced by the 'rule of grace', we must be very careful before we attempt to determine the consequences of anyone's actions.

Week 9

Week 9, Day 1: Matthew 7.3-5

"Why do you see the speck in your neighbor's eye but do not notice the log in your own eye? Or how can you say to your neighbor, 'Let me take the speck out of your eye,' while the log is in your own eye? You hypocrite, first take the log out of your own eye, and then you will see clearly to take the speck out of your neighbor's eye."

Jesus is a wonderful communicator for those who have imagination to picture his parables. In these verses, he tells his disciples a parable to pique their imagination in the area of discernment. The humor in the parable is what makes it work. We are to imagine someone walking around with a two-by-four (that's a two foot by four-foot plank) sticking out of his eye. He sees another person who is blinking continuously and rubbing her eyes to get rid of a tiny speck of sawdust out of her eye. The man approaches her and says, "Here, let me help you get rid of the speck." With a two-by-four protruding from his face, how much can he see? Probably not much! But he is able to see the speck in the woman's eye! Though he can barely see, he has managed to hone in on the woman's tiny flaw.

Jesus calls such a person a hypocrite. This man was able to see the woman's flaw only because he was intent on finding fault. Such a person indicates faults not so that the other person might be better off. After all, the man is in no condition to offer any real help! Rather, finding fault has become an end in itself. This is what Jesus rebukes. This man is a hypocrite because he was hypo-critical about his own faults and hypercritical about the woman's faults.

The Greek word *hypokritês*, normally transliterated "hypocrite," referred to a stage actor, one who puts on a show for others. Hence, the man walking around with the plank in his eye is ignoring it and putting n a show of concern for the woman who has a speck in her eye.

Further, *hypokritês* consists of the preposition *hypo* meaning "under" and the noun *kritês* meaning "judge." Thus, a hypocrite is someone who does not analyze himself or herself enough and who is, therefore, blind to his or her weaknesses or failings.

However, Jesus tells us to be hypercritical about our faults and hypo-critical about others' faults. In other words, we are to treat our faults as seriously as though they were planks protruding from our face and to treat others' faults as though they were inconvenient specks. When we approach others' faults as though they were inconveniences, we cannot condemn them. It would be like damning someone because he or she was ill. Since that is ridiculous, even more ridiculous is damning someone for having a speck in his or her eye.

We must note that Jesus does not tell us not to offer help. He tells the hypocritical person to clean up his act so that he could help the woman. However, we are to offer help with the intent of benefiting each other, not condemning each other. Therefore, to clean up our acts is not to become perfect but to change the attitude with which we correct each other.

Week 9, Day 2: Matthew 7.3-5

"Why do you see the speck in your neighbor's eye but do not notice the log in your own eye? Or how can you say to your neighbor, 'Let me take the speck out of your eye,' while the log is in your own eye? You hypocrite, first take the log out of your own eye, and then you will see clearly to take the speck out of your neighbor's eye."

In the previous devotion, we observed that Jesus tells us to approach others' faults with the attitude of benefiting them. We also briefly noted that Jesus wants us to assist each other. We must keep this in mind. He ends his short parable with the statement, "Then you will see clearly to remove the speck from your brother's or sister's eye." Jesus wants us to provide a helping hand.

To genuinely help someone is not easy. Too often, we offer assistance with an air of superiority. When aiding someone, we easily assume that we are better than the other person. "After all," we say to ourselves, "if the other person were our equal he or she would not need our help!" However, with his use of the word *hypokritês*, Jesus warns us about falling into this trap. All of us are in need of help in some areas or the other. Hence, we are not to consider another person's weaknesses as somehow granting us a superior status.

Then there is always the trap of mutual assistance. We help others with the knowledge that they will help us when we are needy. Rarely do we help those who will never be able to help us. Elsewhere, Jesus will tell his disciples that they should give without any expectation of receiving, that they should even open the doors of their homes for those who would never be able to reciprocate.

Finally, we could have a negative attitude toward the person, offering aid only to disguise our contempt for them. We provide support with an attitude of condemnation. We provide support precisely so that we could remind them later of what a mess they had made of their lives and how they would not be in a better position were it not for us.

Jesus warns us against all of these approaches to providing assistance. To first remove the plank in our eye is to first realize that, far from being better than the other person, we are possibly worse. To remove the obstruction is to recognize that our perception is blurred. To offer assistance after removing the offense in our eye is to have an attitude that recognizes the frailty of all humans—especially ourselves. The hope in all of this is that we critique our own discipleship so that we can then benefit our brother or sister in his or her discipleship.

Once again, we must stress that, because of the parabolic nature of the verses, we should not take them too literally. Jesus is not telling us to become perfect before aiding another Christian. If that were the case, we would have no room for communal living. We would all be isolated followers of Jesus. However, Jesus' thrust in the Sermon on the Mount belies such thinking. We can only follow him insofar as we follow him in the company of others. What Jesus is telling us to do is to recognize that following him is not second nature to us. We constantly struggle to obey him. Once we recognize this, we can better appreciate others' struggles to obey him. With this appreciation we will be better able to offer assistance in the spirit that Jesus advocates.

Week 9, Day 3: Matthew 7.3-5

"Why do you see the speck in your neighbor's eye but do not notice the log in your own eye? Or how can you say to your neighbor, 'Let me take the speck out of your eye,' while the log is in your own eye? You hypocrite, first take the log out of your own eye, and then you will see clearly to take the speck out of your neighbor's eye."

In the previous two devotions, we saw how Jesus tells us we should approach the matter of correcting another Christian. It is crucial for us to recognize that, though he opened the chapter with the words, "Do not judge", he actually goes on to tell us that we should remove the plank in our eye before assisting another Christian to remove a speck from his/her eye.

Jesus' reference to the eye here alludes to his twin utterances earlier in the Sermon. On the one hand he called his disciples 'the light of the world'. However, if one's eye is defective, one will not be able to perceive this light. Hence, just because there is light shining around me, if I am not in a position to receive that light, I will not be able to be guided by it. Specifically here, if I am the person with the plank in my eye, it will obstruct so much light as to render me blind. In this case, I will not be able to recognize the light that other Christians are actually spreading around me.

On the other hand, Jesus warned about having an evil eye. If I have an evil eye, when I look out at the world, I will only be able to see the evil that resides in my heart. In other words, the eye functions as the lens through which the heart perceives in the world what is already in the heart. Hence, it is absolutely crucial for me to identify ways in which I distort my perception of the world on account of the plank that is in my eye.

It is also crucial to remind ourselves that Jesus spoke about the evil eye just before he said we cannot serve both God and money. Money has the ability to distort our perception of the world and of people. Money allows us to turn a blind eye to injustices around us. Money enables us to justify a lot of things that we might not be able to justify if the consideration of money did not hang around our necks. We will look at the dangerous effects of money in the summary devotions that I will write after we complete chapter 7.

But for now, I wish to explore what having a plank in

my eye would actually do. Contrary to some common understandings of biblical interpretation, we all come to the text with presuppositions that guide our interpretation and influence our understanding of God and how he deals with the world. Having a plank in my eye affects how I view the world and will affect how I interpret the scriptures. In other words, my having a plank in my eyes will result in my having a distorted understanding of God because God will have to be the one who created the world that I perceive.

What this means is that removing the plank from my eye is not just a crucial step *before* I can help someone else. Rather, it is also a crucial step *before* I reach a reasonable understanding of the character and nature of God. After all, if I am not able to see well enough to even know how another human needs assistance, how can I presume to know *anything* reliable about God as long as the plank is still in my eye? Hence, we can see another reason why Jesus tells us to treat our failings with utmost seriousness, even though he does not make it explicit here.

"Do not give what is holy to dogs, and do not throw your pearls before swine, or they will trample them under foot and turn and maul you."

Our natural tendency is to think that we are right and that, therefore, someone else must be wrong. We easily think that Jesus must be warning us about others. He must be warning us about "dogs" and "pigs," people who do not deserve or understand God's riches. So we focus our energy on determining who these "pigs" and "dogs" might be. Are they unbelievers? Are they Gentiles? Are they backslidden Christians?

Another common inclination is to think of Jesus as the dispenser of treasures and holy things. We then devote our resources to understanding what the "pearls" or "sacred things" might be. Is it the gospel? Is it an understanding of deeper mysteries of the faith like the doctrine of the Trinity or the dual natures of Jesus or the gifts and fruit of the Spirit?

The power of Jesus' words lies in understanding them

against our predispositions. To do that, we must first understand the context of this verse. In the preceding few devotions, we have seen Jesus telling his disciples to assist each other generously. We are not to condemn each other, but are to discern proper from improper discipleship. We are to recognize our own frailty when we help others. Given the strong words Jesus uses, recognition of our frailty could easily lead us to think that we can escape responsibility for our actions if we let others indulge their improper actions. After all, when Jesus says, "In the same way you judge others, you will be judged," does he not mean that if we overlook others' sins, God will overlook ours?

How crooked we can be! Therefore, Jesus adds this terse verse. Rather than focus on the treasures or to whom it is given, we need to concentrate on the one who gives the treasures. The devastating power of Jesus' words lies in the realization that someone who gives pearls to pigs and sacred things to dogs is primarily responsible for not understanding the value of the treasure. After all, if I knew that a string of pearls I had was worth a fortune, would I give it to my dog as a plaything?

Jesus tells us that if we overlook others' sins with the

understanding that God will overlook our sins, we are the ones who do not understand the true worth of God's forgiveness. This is what Dietrich Bonhoeffer called "cheap grace." Cheap grace is grace that is offered cheaply. Cheap grace is grace that ignores the cost of discipleship. In other words, Jesus is telling us that if we offer forgiveness without the cost of repentance and transformation, we reveal an impoverished view of grace.

This is very important. There is a quite common assumption in Christian circles that forgiveness means just forgetting or overlooking the past. We must, however, recognize that there are different levels of forgiveness. When Jesus asks the Father to forgive those who were crucifying him, he is asking the Father not to hold the crime against them. However, there is no restoration of any relationship involved. Yet, when Jesus interacts with Peter after the resurrection, asking him if he loved him, there is a restoration of the relationship.

The goal of forgiveness should always be the restoration of the relationship, as far as possible. However, if we offer forgiveness without the expectation of repentance and transformation, we are actually saying that we do not care about the person. In other words, when we offer a shallow version of 'forgiveness', we demonstrate that we haven't actually understood what forgiveness entails. We do not understand that forgiveness, ultimately, is concerned about the restoration of relationships and the development of *shalom* in the world. We are then like foolish people who give pearls to pigs and what is holy to dogs.

"Do not judge so that you will not be judged. For by the standard you judge you will be judged, and the measure you use will be the measure you receive. Why do you see the speck in your neighbor's eye but do not notice the log in your own eye? Or how can you say to your neighbor, 'Let me take the speck out of your eye,' while the log is in your own eye? You hypocrite, first take the log out of your own eye, and then you will see clearly to take the speck out of your neighbor's eye. Do not give what is holy to dogs, and do not throw your pearls before swine, or they will trample them under foot and turn and maul you."

Discipleship is a communal effort. No one can be a solitary Christian. Moreover, if we are honest, we will admit that following Jesus is not easy. We need others to guide us. We need the help of other Christians for all of us have blind spots in which we do not recognize our failure to follow Jesus. We need others also to encourage us.

However, if following Jesus is not easy, the part of discipleship that deals with encouraging and correcting each other is probably the hardest. We are plagued with two extreme ills. On the one hand, we can have a superior air and look down on other Christians. We will have an over critical approach due to which we are able to spot only others' failures. On the other hand, we may recognize our frailty and find in that an excuse for sinful practices. We will have an *hypo*-critical approach resulting in our overlooking others' sinful behavior with the hope that they and God would overlook our sinful behavior.

Both these extremes are to be avoided. Healthy discipleship lies in the middle ground between these two extremes. Healthy discipleship begins with a robust view of God's grace and forgiveness. We recognize that God's forgiveness works in those who realize their sinfulness. We then recognize that all Christians, ourselves included, are frail sinners. We understand that God's grace includes the empowerment to struggle with and overcome sinful behavior. Moreover, we appreciate that most of all God's grace is the call to follow Jesus.

To those who have received this gracious call Jesus advocates the middle ground. In this middle ground, we entertain neither harsh judgmentalism nor cozy licentiousness. Rather, we embrace the call to discerning forgiveness and forgiving discernment—the marks of Jesus' followers.

In this middle ground, we also recognize that forgiveness cannot be synonymous with 'cheap grace'. Neither can it depend on an 'as you sow, so you reap' mentality. Forgiveness is costly, but not driven by any idea of just deserts. In fact, it is precisely those whom we may think do not deserve forgiveness who need it the most. It is precisely those who have lost face who need to be shown forgiveness. In recognizing the fact that we are called to forgive those whom we would think are outside the purview of our forgiveness, we are enabled to realize how precious forgiveness is. In that case, we will treat it as something precious, neither hoarding it nor offering it without a thought.

"Ask, and it will be given to you; search, and you will find; knock, and the door will be opened for you. For everyone who asks receives, and everyone who searches finds, and for everyone who knocks, the door will be opened."

These verses raise three important questions: For what may we pray? What should be our attitude in prayer? What may we expect prayer to accomplish? Let us deal with each of these questions in turn.

So what things may we ask for and for what may we not? In v. 11 Jesus tells us that the "Father in heaven will give good things to those who ask him!" Does this not mean that we should ask only for 'good things'? Not so! Jesus encourages us to ask for anything, while he promises us that God will respond by giving us 'good things'. The important thing to realize is that Jesus is fully aware that humans do not know what is good. If he were to tell us to ask only for 'good things', we would pause to decide if a given request is good or not. We would spend more time deciding if we should pray for something than actually praying!

If we have any doubts that Jesus knows that humans do not know what is good, we need only look at him at Gethsemane. In Matthew 26.39, Jesus prays, "My Father, if it is possible, let this cup pass from me." Though Jesus had previously been convinced that his going to the cross was good, at Gethsemane he is in anguish and the issue gets blurred. He asks for the same thing for which he had earlier (16.21-23) chastised Peter! There, Peter had said that suffering was not a part of the Messiah's vocation. And here Jesus asks precisely for the cup of suffering to be taken from him. Jesus does not skip the request. He could well have said, "Father, let what you want happen." If he did take such an approach, we might well ask what the purpose of such a prayer might be. Indeed, to be able to yield to God's will—especially when it runs against ours—is to know and fully articulate before God what our will is. Without knowing that what we want might be different from what God wants, we will not be able to surrender joyfully to God's will.

When Jesus tells us, "Ask, and you will receive," the last thing he would have us do is contemplate if a request is appropriate. He tells us that a request made to God is always appropriate. Let me repeat so that this point is taken. We can ask God for anything without restriction. We are not supposed to ponder if what we are asking for is 'good' or not.

However, what about the line of thinking that warns us to be careful what we ask for, lest God grants our request? To be frank, such thinking has no place in Jesus' view. God will give us only 'good things'. God is not a dispenser of bad things. To make the words with which Jesus encourages prayer into a warning about prayer itself is to mutilate Jesus' teachings. To make God's giving nature the reason to hesitate in prayer is to misunderstand that very nature. We do not have to be careful when praying. We do not have to weigh the pros and cons of our prayers. For Jesus tells us, "Ask, seek, knock," for when God responds, it will only be with 'good things'.

Many of us have made requests, earnest requests, only to receive a firm, "No!" from God. We are not supposed to ask ourselves if what we requested was 'good' or not. However, Jesus encourages us to consider God's response as being 'good'. We may not be able to understand how some specific response might be 'good'. In fact, we may never understand before our deaths. However, Jesus encourages us to trust that God's response, no matter what it is, no matter how inscrutable, no matter how bizarre, no matter how outlandish, will be 'good'.

254

Week 9, Day 7: Matthew 7.7-8

"Ask, and it will be given to you; search, and you will find; knock, and the door will be opened for you. For everyone who asks receives, and everyone who searches finds, and for everyone who knocks, the door will be opened."

Having addressed the issue of what we may pray for, let us consider what our attitude should be in prayer. "Ask," says Jesus, "and you will receive." Jesus is making it clear to us that God both hears and answers prayer. Prayer is not a way of speaking our needs to the wind. Rather, it is speaking to the only person who is fully able to answer us.

Prayer, like most spiritual disciplines, is paradoxical. On the one hand, it is powerlessness, because in prayer we acknowledge our impotence. On the other hand, it is empowering, because prayer is directed to God, who is able to alter our situation and who is positively disposed toward us as his children. The upshot of this paradox is that we are to pray expecting God to grant our request. Prayer should be a source of hope rather than a way of fueling hopelessness.

This does not mean that we need to ask only once before God answers our request. That may be the case on a given occasion. However, it is not true in general. As a principle, we need to persevere in prayer. Most often, we need to ask until we receive the answer to our prayer.

But note that Jesus does not promise that we will receive what we asked for. He only says, "Everyone who asks receives." We might be tempted to think that this is some sort of formula. And indeed there are many false teachers who tell their followers that this is what the verse means. However, any view of our relationship with God that attempts to force or tie God's hands is inherently unloving and, therefore, not something that Jesus would ever advocate.

However, once we realize that we have encountered a paradox, we must wonder how we are to hold together these seemingly disparate ways of praying. How can we expect a response while expecting to make the request again? What we need to do is pray one prayer at a time. That is, every time we pray, we should pray as though this were the time when God would answer. Just as we are not to hoard treasures in physical storehouses, so also we must not hoard prayers for later. Each time we pray, we should empty the store of prayers we have.

Each day, when we are done praying, it should be when we are unable to pray more either because we have run out of things for which to pray or because we have dissipated all the expectancy we had before beginning to pray. When we do this we can pray with anticipation and we can pray without ceasing. Indeed, as long as we have not received a clear conviction from God that we should stop praying for a particular thing, our requests for that thing will be truly expectant only if we pray repeatedly and will be truly persistent only if we pray with the hope of receiving a response.

It is not an easy task to juggle both expectation and perseverance. However, this is what the life of faith eventually requires of us. At some stage we will reach a point where the response from God is unclear or delayed. In such a situation, we are to keep asking and seeking and knocking.

At the same time, we should avoid the temptation to showcase ourselves as having superior faith by welcoming whatever response we get as though it were exactly what we asked for. This tendency among Christians to take *any* response as exactly the response we hoped for, without expressing bewilderment or disappointment actually is not a sign of strong faith but of a dysfunctional relationship with God in which we believe God is unable to handle our own honest interpretation of his response to our prayer.

Week 10

Week 10, Day 1: Matthew 7.7-8

"Ask, and it will be given to you; search, and you will find; knock, and the door will be opened for you. For everyone who asks receives, and everyone who searches finds, and for everyone who knocks, the door will be opened."

In the previous two devotions, we have seen that Jesus teaches us to pray for anything. He tells us that, since God gives only 'good things', we do not need to determine if we are praying for 'good things', but can leave the decision to God.. Jesus also teaches us to be persistent and expectant in prayer.

However, we could probably cite many examples of people who prayed boldly and expectantly, whose prayers went unanswered. How then can Jesus say, "Everyone who asks, receives; everyone who seeks, finds; and to one who knocks the door will be opened"? Is that not a blatant falsehood? In fact, for people who have prayed earnestly and have seen their requests denied, Jesus' words would be a slap in the face. After all, their unanswered prayers leave them vulnerable to the charge that if they did not receive, they probably did not ask! That is, they probably did not ask with the right attitude, or with the right words, or with adequate faith. And how many of us have contributed to their wounds by targeting them with just such arguments?

However, have we considered the possibility that Jesus might say, "Everyone who asks, receives" knowing well that not everyone who asks receives? Before you dismiss this idea, let us look at Proverbs 16.3: "Commit to the Lord whatever you do, and your plans will succeed." We know from experience that this is not always true. We can cite personal examples of plans that failed despite our dependence on God.

In the spirit of Old Testament proverbs, Jesus makes a sweeping generalization. The goal of this is not to give some universal truth. Rather, it is a way of getting people to recognize what is important. In the case of Jesus' words, our relationship of dependence on God is more important than God's giving us everything we requested. However, getting what we ask for is important to us. Hence, Jesus promises us answers if we engage in what is really important—prayer!

Is this a carrot on a stick? In some ways it is. Jesus

offers us incentives if we pray. Jesus capitalizes on our narrow focus to get us to have a broader perspective. However, in some ways, this is not a carrot on a stick. Our prayers are often answered. We do regularly receive what we ask for. Not always! But regularly. We understand Jesus' intent best when we realize that he says these words not to give us a formula for twisting God's arm, but to encourage us to pray!

As we saw yesterday, this does not mean that we *always* receive what we ask for, that we *always* find what we seek for, or that we *always* have the door on which we knocked open for us. What then is Jesus getting at through these words? What he is saying is that we always receive when we ask, but not necessarily what we asked for; we always find when we seek, but not always what we sought; we always find a door opening, but not always the one on which we knocked. We are often disappointed in prayer. However, the life of faith is one in which we develop, despite all the disappointments, an unshakeable trust in the goodness of God. Whatever we receive, whatever we find, whatever door swings open, it is good even though, at the time, every ounce of our being may rebel against taking it in that way.

Week 10, Day 2: Matthew 7.9-11

"Is there anyone among you who, if his son asks for bread, will give him a stone? Or if he asks for a fish, will give him a snake? If you then, although you are evil, know how to give good gifts to your children, how much more will your Father in heaven give good gifts to those who ask him!"

Having instructed his disciples to pray persistently, Jesus provides an additional reason for persistence in prayer. This time around, however, Jesus employs the absurd. "Which of you…" he asks, knowing full well that the absurdities he describes would lead each of his hearers to say, "Not me!" The power of Jesus' words lies in the realization that no person would consciously admit to giving his or her child a snake instead of a fish. Few parents would publicly admit to being rotten parents! Jesus' words work because almost all parents who hear these words will have the gut reaction, "Not me!"

Having moved his audience to respond with their gut, Jesus makes his argument. He tells us that all humans are 'evil'. Contrary to some strands of Christian thought that propose humans are totally depraved, this does not mean that there is no good bone in us! Rather, it means that we are not thoroughly good. We are stained with what is not good, with what is evil. Once we understand that this is what Jesus means, few of us would object to his evaluation. We know that, though we may be good for the most part, we are not good all the time. There are times—if not most times—when we act from impure motives. We are selfish. We indulge unjust anger. We are greedy. All of these traits make it difficult to reject Jesus' evaluation.

Jesus then makes his point. If people who are selfish and greedy can respond selflessly and generously to their children, should we not expect that God, who is at heart selfless and generous, would respond to his children with greater selflessness and generosity? The benevolence of human parents underscores the abundance of God's provisions.

Unfortunately, we do know of parents who respond inappropriately to their children. Neglect and abuse are sadly common. How would a person who suffered parental neglect and abuse respond to Jesus' words? Someone who was starved, beaten, or molested might be disinclined to accept Jesus' portrait of God. Insecurity in the presence of one's parents might evoke insecurity in God's presence. In light of this, how do we proceed?

Once again, the power of Jesus' words lies in the fact that abusive parents would publicly lie about their parental abuse. They would cover up their horrendous acts, thereby revealing the impropriety of their relationship to their children. Abused children, observing their parent's duplicity, are enabled to recognize that the abuse is wrong. They are empowered to reject the idea that they deserve the abuse. That Jesus does this in the name of God's benevolent parenthood then becomes a challenge to people abused by their parents to test God's parenting. In other words, Jesus says, "The abuse you received at the hands of your parents was wrong. God says that it is wrong. I invite you to experience God's parenting. You will find that he will not mistreat you because he is good through and through."

But Jesus' words also relate to those of us who had good, well meaning parents. Even the best intentioned parents would have done something that wasn't quite ok. No parent has ever been completely perfect as a parent. However, in this case, their good intentions are an indication of what we should expect from God. God, as our Father, not only intends the best for us, but also knows what is best for us. Hence, when we receive something from God, we should develop the trust of accepting that, though it may be something extremely harrowing, since it comes from our Father, it must be good.

I know that this is not easy to accept, even intellectually, let alone in our hearts. We have some ideas of what might be 'good' in our lives. However, we should recognize that we do not have a broad enough perspective to determine beyond doubt what might actually be 'good' for us.

At the same time, when we receive something that is harrowing from God, we can only continue in trust if we also believe that he is accompanying us and experiencing what we are going through. A spectator God cannot be trusted because he excuses himself from the pain he puts us through. But a co-suffering God can be trusted because he shows us that he will not even spare himself in order to bond with us in our suffering. Just as a well intentioned parent will not turn his/her back on the suffering of his/her child, but will attempt to understand what hurts the child, so also the co-suffering God faces the difficulties with us and in so doing understands what we are going through.

Week 10, Day 3: Matthew 7.12

"In everything, treat others as you would want them to treat you, for this fulfills the law and the prophets."

This verse is often called "The Golden Rule." Some early Christian interpreters thought that this verse could be misused and they warned against it. They claimed, for instance, that people could throw extravagant banquets in the hope that others would do the same for them. They could overlook others' sins hoping that others would respond likewise. However, in the context of the Sermon on the Mount, such thinking reveals an underlying misunderstanding of the Sermon. One of the main goals of the Sermon is to get the hearer to emulate God's generosity. God is lavish without expecting even our gratitude. Jesus hopes that we would become like that.

I would go so far as to say that, if my method of interpreting any of Jesus' words results in my deciding that I should not teach others to adhere to what he says, then my method of interpretation is suspect. I wish Christian interpreters held to this principle *before* attempting to understand any passage that involves Jesus' teachings.

A closer examination, however, of Jesus' phrasing of the Golden Rule reveals that the deviant thinking exemplified in the opening paragraph of this devotion is positively excluded. Jesus does not say, "Do things for others so that they would do the same for you." Rather, consistent with his emphasis through the Sermon, Jesus asks us to place ourselves in others' shoes. If we were needy, we would want to be recipients of others' generosity. If we were guilty of some serious sin, we would desire others' forgiveness. If someone helped us, we would like him or her to be discreet about it. So Jesus tells us that we should be generous, forgiving, and discreet.

In other words, in the context of the Sermon on the Mount, the Golden Rule is not some universal principle that we can act on as we wish. In the preceding portions of the Sermon, Jesus has given us instructions about specific circumstances. However, we can easily recognize that he does not cover the whole gamut of our experience. Therefore, the Golden Rule functions as a challenge to act appropriately in all circumstances. The examples Jesus gives us in the Sermon should show us how to understand the Golden Rule in other instances.

Therefore, we need to understand that what Jesus is engendering through the Golden Rule is maturity in his disciples. He does not give us a detailed manual on how to live life. That would take away from us any sense of responsibility for our actions. After all, if Jesus told us what to do in a situation, he is the one responsible for our actions! However, Jesus entrusts us with the indispensable task of struggling daily to determine what might be the 'golden' way of acting in our specific circumstances. In this way, we are held responsible for what we do. In this way, we realize the immense cost of discipleship and mature as disciples.

What Jesus does through the Golden Rule is tell us that we are responsible creatures, created to be God's images in the world. We do not need an external arbiter for our behavior, but know in our bones the difference between right and wrong. All we need to do is put ourselves in the other person's shoes. Jesus, therefore, tells us that it is impossible to be his disciple without also inculcating in ourselves the ability to empathize with others. Actually, since Jesus is restoring for us the true way of being human, I would go so far as to say that it is impossible to be human without developing in ourselves the ability to empathize with others. In other words, rather than being a vapid call to some spiritualized quid pro quo, the Golden Rule is about empathy.

"Ask and it will be given to you; seek and you will find; knock and it will be opened for you. For everyone who asks receives, and the one who seeks finds, and to the one who knocks it will be opened. Or what man is there among you, if his son will ask him for bread, will give him a stone? Or also if he will ask for a fish, will give him a snake? Therefore if you, although you are evil, know how to give good gifts to your children, how much more will your Father who is in heaven give good things to those who ask him? Therefore in all things, whatever you want that people should do to you, thus also you do to them. For this is the law and the prophets."

If, after hearing or reading the Lord's Prayer, we had any doubt that prayer implies actions, Jesus dispels this doubt in Matthew 7.7-12. We are to pray persistently with the promise that God will hear and answer us. Jesus even tells us that the benevolence of human parents should convince us of God's benevolence.

However, Jesus ends this section on asking, seeking, and knocking with the Golden Rule, which emphasizes our actions. Jesus does this because actions bring to light our convictions. If we act contrary to the Golden Rule, we reveal that, when we pray, we do not think of God as generous and lavish. To act contrary to the Golden Rule is to betray the fact that we believe we pray to a miserly God.

On the other hand, believing that God is munificent will result in our praying persistently for him to act magnanimously in our lives so that we can then act in like manner toward others. Moreover, believing that God is bountiful will motivate us to struggle to live out the Golden Rule. In other words, God's benevolence is the glue that fuses prayer and action.

No longer then may we entertain the idea that we can pray without acting. Neither may we consider the possibility of acting without praying. Both these options can only arise from a conviction that God is tightfisted. The only option for Jesus' disciples is to pray and act. Indeed, the Golden Rule containing the words 'do to others' is addressed specifically to those who have already heard the words 'ask', 'seek', and 'knock'.

Jesus does not allow us to entertain the idea that we can have a relationship with the Father, symbolized by the words 'ask', 'seek', and 'knock', without also having a similar relationship with others, symbolized by the Golden Rule. It is unfortunate, and a sign of how far the Church has strayed from the teachings of Jesus, that there are huge swathes of Christians who think that the Christian life is one characterized by a 'me and Jesus' attitude. To be very specific, in light of the two preeminent commands, we can say that 'asking', 'seeking', and 'knocking' are ways in which we demonstrate our love for God by trusting him to be generous in his responses to our prayers, and that the Golden Rule is the way in which we demonstrate our love for our neighbor. Of course, the two are joined in this passage by Jesus' words about the generosity and goodness of God. God's goodness and generosity are what fuels our love for him and our love for our neighbors. And as James says, it is impossible to have one without the other.

Week 10, Day 5: Matthew 7.13-14

"Enter through the narrow gate, for the gate is wide and the road is easy that leads to destruction, and there are many who take it. For the gate is narrow and the road is hard that leads to life, and there are few who find it."

Since these verses come right after the Golden Rule, we need to understand them in light of it. Jesus is telling us that bringing to life the Golden Rule is difficult. While the rule may encapsulate the best of religious wisdom, and while most people might acknowledge that it does, following the rule runs contrary to our inclinations. Few indeed choose to give it expression in practical terms. However, Jesus challenges us to do just that.

It is important to observe that Jesus is not talking about having the right doctrine. The narrow gate should be understood in terms of Jesus' focus in the Sermon on the Mount. Jesus is telling us that obedience to him is not easy. The Greek word *stenos*, normally translated 'narrow', actually means 'crowded', 'cramped', 'confined', or 'restricted'. In other words, the focus is not on the road but on the experience of those on the road. Keeping this in mind, we might say that obedience to Jesus cramps our style! This is not to say that when we follow Jesus, we will be misunderstood or persecuted. That is likely true. However, that is not Jesus' point. Rather, when we obey Jesus, he leads us to make decisions that reduce our options and restrict our actions.

In other words, Jesus himself restricts his disciples. They are no longer at liberty to hate their enemies. They do not have his permission to retaliate violently. They are to take marriage with utmost seriousness. The list goes on! When we follow Jesus, he asks us to burn bridges behind us. He expects us to preclude some courses of action. This naturally calls into question something we often take for granted—our freedom.

Here we must observe that Jesus does not say that in surrendering our freedom to him we will experience freedom. Indeed, if anything, he is saying the opposite! He is telling us that, when we follow him, we will experience the loss of freedom. The road he will have us walk will be restricted because we will experience it to be restricted. We will experience it to be restricted precisely because we will know that there are options of which we may not avail, but of which others may. Dietrich Bonhoeffer recognizes this when he writes, "To confess and testify to the truth as it is in Jesus, and at the same time to love the enemies of that truth, his enemies and ours, and to love them with the infinite love of Jesus Christ, is indeed a narrow way."

Once again, it is important to stress that Jesus' words here have nothing to do with our being persecuted or misunderstood. This has nothing to do with how others respond to us. Others may very well respond in an adversarial manner to our being Jesus' disciples. However, this is not what Jesus is getting at. Rather, he is clearly saying that he is the one who refuses to allow his disciples some options that those who aren't his disciples may feel free to consider. The restriction that we experience is on account of his character and the nature of his kingdom. Some options just do not fit well with the ethos of his kingdom. These options are excluded from the repertoire of a Christian, as a result of which we experience being constrained.

"Enter through the narrow gate, for the gate is wide and the road is easy that leads to destruction, and there are many who take it. For the gate is narrow and the road is hard that leads to life, and there are few who find it."

Very often these words are taken as Jesus' teaching about the relative 'traffic' of people headed to heaven and hell. Hence, we often hear it said that there is a stairway to heaven and a highway to hell, indicating that very few people get to heaven while the vast majority are sent to hell.

Before we proceed to deal with the implications of Jesus' words, which we will do tomorrow, let us consider what such a claim would mean about God. Let's say that 60% of people wind up in the 'bad place' while 40% are welcomed into the 'good place'. I am intentionally not using the words 'hell' and 'heaven' because they carry too much baggage - baggage that is not just *not* derived from the bible but also that presents a deficient understanding of God and a truncated vision of what it means to be human. Now a 60-40 split certainly does not account for the highway-stairway contrast. However, let us entertain this split for now.

What this means is that, out of 10 people God creates, 6 of them wind up in the 'bad place' and, traditionally, once a person is sent to the 'bad place' he/she is there permanently. Does this not mean that God has failed in his purposes for these 6 people? After all, we read that God desires all people to be saved. In this scenario, God has a loss rate of 60%. In what warped method of calculation can this be considered a symbol of God's victory? Moreover, if we consider that the bible teaches us that 'God is love', in what sense can the acceptance of a 60% loss be counted as loving? If one is going to lose so much, why bother initiating this game?

If we take either the view that God predestines everyone (i.e. the Augustinian or Calvinist view) or that God foreknows everyone's choices (i.e. the Arminian view), we reach the same conclusion. God knows *before* he starts creation who is going to end up in the 'good place' and who in the 'bad place'. This means that, for the majority who wind up in the 'bad place', God created them knowing that they would be condemned and punished without end. Quite frankly, anyone who can claim that a god who did this is loving either has a different definition of 'love' than I do or has a different 'god' in mind than I do, or more likely both.

Now, I may be wrong in my understanding of God and of love. But we must be honest and admit that, even if I am wrong, the person who thinks that a god who can knowingly consign so many people to the 'bad place' is 'loving' has a different understanding of God and of love than I have.[17]

But let us assume I am not too far off in my understanding of God and love. In that case, it would be impossible for a loving God to create humans if he knew that the majority would end up in the 'bad place'. However, we know that God has created humans! Hence, it must be true that the majority of humans *do not* end up in the 'bad place'.

However, Jesus does talk about the 'narrow gate' and the 'wide gate', the 'hard road' and the 'easy road', one leading to life, the other to destruction and few finding the former. Yet, if this cannot lead to the conclusion that most humans will wind up in the 'bad place', we must conclude that he is talking about something completely different than what is traditionally

---

[17] Now, if someone has this other view of God and love, I will be talking past that person because we are using the same words to mean quite different things. However, this is not the place for debate. If someone wishes to debate this matter, I welcome it. Please email me at deepakmbabu@gmail.com.

supposed. What might that be? Stay tuned!

279

Week 10, Day 7: Matthew 7.13-14

"Enter through the narrow gate, for the gate is wide and the road is easy that leads to destruction, and there are many who take it. For the gate is narrow and the road is hard that leads to life, and there are few who find it."

Previously, in this series of devotions, we realized that assuming these verses assert that only a few people will enter the 'good place' while most will enter the 'bad place' leads to the conclusion that God cannot be loving. So how do we unravel the mystery behind these verses? Actually, the mystery has been introduced precisely because most Christians do not reflect on what their doctrines say about the character of God.

Now, if these verses have nothing to do with who is or who is not going to the 'good place', what might they be about? We should note that, contrary to the claim that Jesus speaks a lot about the 'bad place' (i.e. 'hell'), this is not the case. It is only the case if we assume that *gehenna* should be translated as 'hell' and that 'hell' refers to a place where people are tormented endlessly. However, Jesus rarely, if ever, focuses on that. He is concerned not about some destination ('good place' or 'bad place') 'in the sweet by and by', but about our imitation of him in the here and now.

Now, Matthew does use the word *apóleia*, which is often translated as 'destruction'. However, we deny what Jesus is trying to do, namely enable us to be conformed into his image, if we think this is a reference to some sort of never ending punishment! Since we have been conformed to a different way of understanding these verses, allow me to give an illustration.

If I fill a car with a diesel engine full of petrol, I will destroy the diesel engine in the here and now! It's not something that will happen in the sweet by and by! The engine is designed to operate with diesel now. Filling it with petrol now and hoping for diesel in the future is completely pointless. Indeed, if I fill it with something for which it is not designed, I will be destroying it.

Humans are designed to image God. But, as the New Testament insists, the perfect revelation of God is given to us through Jesus. Hence, we are designed to follow the way of Jesus, with its demands of fidelity, forgiveness, nonviolence, generosity, humility, etc. If we act in ways that deny this, we deny our nature. We will then destroy ourselves and become less able to fulfill the vocation for which God has created us.

If this is true, then we can see that the common interpretation of these verses as referring to the 'good place' and the 'bad place' actually undermines our ability to fulfill our vocation as God's images by distracting us and drawing our focus away from the task at hand. But if we remember that Jesus is focused on the here and now, then we can see what he is saying.

What he is saying is that the path he presents to us is odious to most humans. Yes, I used the word 'odious' intentionally to highlight how abhorrent we think it is. In fact, so odious is this path that the Church has replaced the reference to it with an empty in the sweet by and by hope! Yes, the Church itself has found the vision presented by Jesus odious and has, for the most part, rejected it.

This is precisely why Jesus has to tell us that there are few who find the 'narrow path'. And it pays to remember that Jesus is not talking to some random group of outsiders, but to those who wanted to follow him. Indeed, Matthew introduces the Sermon on the Mount with the words, "When Jesus saw the crowds, he went up the mountain, and after he sat down, *his disciples came to him*. And he began to speak and taught them." The Sermon on the Mount is his first teaching *to his disciples* and it is to them that he says, "The gate is narrow and the road is hard that leads to life, and there are few who find it," precisely because they are the ones most likely to reject the message!

In other words, *even among his disciples*, there are few who find the constricted road that leads to life. That this is true is clear from the way the Church has systematically undermined Jesus' own words about this by relegating them to a distant future when it is clear from everything he says in the Sermon that it is about discipleship in this life.

Week 11

Week 11, Day 1: Matthew 7.15-20

"Beware of false prophets, who come to you in sheep's clothing but inwardly are ravenous wolves. You will know them by their fruits. Are grapes gathered from thorns or figs from thistles? In the same way, every good tree bears good fruit, but the bad tree bears bad fruit. A good tree cannot bear bad fruit, nor can a bad tree bear good fruit. Every tree that does not bear good fruit will be cut down and thrown into the fire. Thus you will know them by their fruits."

After a general warning about the difficulty of discipleship, Jesus issues a warning about leaders. His words of caution against 'false prophets' naturally motivate us to define what would qualify someone as a false prophet. Often, the criterion of correct doctrine is suggested. Unfortunately, this has led to quite virulent divisions among Christians. 'Orthodox' people have said that 'heretics' were the false prophets and the 'heretics' have returned the favor. Indeed, the criterion of doctrine can only lead to increasingly restrictive doctrinal positions, as more and more people are considered heretical. The desire for purity—in this case, doctrinal purity—is doomed to fail if done in terms of eliminating what is impure. There must, therefore, be another way forward.

Before moving on, we must make a few observations. Jesus tells us that the false prophets address him as Lord and do miracles in his name. Presumably, they are Christians. Moreover, they also have supernatural gifts. In other words, the false prophets are indistinguishable from other Christians on both confessional and ministerial grounds. Indeed Jesus does not rebuke false prophets on these grounds. Also, Jesus' statement about these leaders' being 'ravenous wolves' does not mean that false prophets necessarily have destructive motives. We will address this in tomorrow's devotion.

What Jesus warns us about is their 'fruit'. While this is a clue, Jesus' incorporation of the image in his short parable about trees and fruit makes it difficult to interpret. Indeed, failure to recognize the parable could lead us to think that Jesus is talking about evangelism and church growth. However, Jesus' use of the image indicates that 'fruit' is to be seen as the outward manifestation of what lies inside a person. Given the thrust of the Sermon, it is best to view 'fruit' in terms of public response to Jesus' teachings. A person who obeys yields good fruit. A disobedient person produces bad fruit. We will return to the metaphor of fruit the day after tomorrow, after our look at the metaphor of 'ravenous wolves' tomorrow.

While Jesus' words are specifically directed toward those who are leaders, we dare not restrict his words only to those who hold official leadership positions within the Church. Jesus is certainly addressing pastors and priests and deacons and bishops, etc. However, he is not addressing only them. After all, earlier in the Sermon he said, "Therefore, whoever breaks one of the least of these commandments and teaches others to do the same will be called least in the kingdom of heaven, but whoever does them and teaches them will be called great in the kingdom of heaven." In other words, anyone who is in a position to wield any level of influence over how other Christians live is held responsible by Jesus. And since he has already told us, "First take the log out of your own eye, and then you will see clearly to take the speck out of your neighbor's eye," he envisions a thoroughly integrated body of believers where each person is responsible to and for everyone else, thereby being in a position to influence everyone else and, therefore, qualifying himself/herself as a 'teacher' or 'prophet'.

Week 11, Day 2: Matthew 7.15-20

"Beware of false prophets, who come to you in sheep's clothing but inwardly are ravenous wolves. You will know them by their fruits. Are grapes gathered from thorns or figs from thistles? In the same way, every good tree bears good fruit, but the bad tree bears bad fruit. A good tree cannot bear bad fruit, nor can a bad tree bear good fruit. Every tree that does not bear good fruit will be cut down and thrown into the fire. Thus you will know them by their fruits."

Jesus uses some quite sharp words when he calls false prophets 'ravenous wolves'. This metaphor is powerful and needs careful attention. In yesterday's devotion I claimed that, though Jesus uses this strong metaphor, this does not mean that the false prophets have destructive motives.

You see, a wolf is an apex predator. That is its nature. When it kills an animal, it is not intending 'destruction' of the animal. Rather, it is just hunting to feed itself. Of course, there have been cases where wolves have behaved out of character, as it were. However, just as we should not judge humans by our worst examples, we should not judge the wolves by the individual wolves that displayed aberrant behavior. In general, wolves function as predators without intending destruction.

This is the power behind what Jesus is saying. He is not saying that 'false prophets' are Christian leaders with evil intentions or bad character. In fact, that is precisely *not* what he is warning us about. This is because, when people are intentionally destructive, it is relatively easy to spot them and remove ourselves from the circle of their influence.

Far more devastating is the 'false prophet' who genuinely believes he/she is speaking for God. Such a person actually thinks he/she is leading the people in ways that facilitate genuine discipleship while actually being a hindrance to them. Such a teacher points to the wide road and says that it is narrow because they have misunderstood what Jesus actually means when he refers to the narrow road. Such a person misidentifies his/her priorities for Jesus' priorities and substitutes Jesus' priorities with his/her own, thereby making those who follow him/her focus on what Jesus would want us to ignore and to ignore what Jesus would want us to focus on. Because he/she has misunderstood what Jesus is getting at, he/she cannot but be the one through whom those who follow him/her wind up on the wide road that leads to their destruction.

There are many Christian teachers, and I hope I am not one, who have the best of intentions, but who, because they fail to understand that the revelation that comes to us in and through Jesus supersedes all other revelation, often prioritize some teaching in the bible while ignoring or abrogating Jesus' teachings. This often happens under the umbrella of twin ideas that are very common among Christians.

The first is the assumption that there are no contradictions in the bible. If there are no contradictions then we can take a teaching anywhere else in the bible and conclude that Jesus *must* surely be teaching something aligned with the other teaching. However, if the bible speaks with multiple voices and there are contradictions, then we can accept that Jesus might be teaching something at odds with something clearly taught in some other part of the bible and have no qualms saying that, since we are *Christians*, who supposedly follow Jesus, we will accept his teaching and reject the teaching that contradicts him.

The second is the assumption that scripture interprets

scripture. While this sounds great on paper, it is based on the first false assumption that scripture cannot and does not speak with multiple voices. However, now that we are forced to believe there are no contradictions, we have to *explain away* one of the teachings. Since we always come to scripture with our own life experiences and priorities, what eventually happens is that we accept what we find easier to live out. We then assume that the passage that teaches what we find easier to live out is the clearer passage and the other passage is the difficult passage that needs to be interpreted in light of the easier passage. We will then find excuses not to obey Jesus when he says things like, "Love your enemies," not because Jesus is unclear but because we cannot bring ourselves to love our enemies and so conclude that this could surely not be what Jesus meant.

Week 11, Day 3: Matthew 7.15-20

"Beware of false prophets, who come to you in sheep's clothing but inwardly are ravenous wolves. You will know them by their fruits. Are grapes gathered from thorns or figs from thistles? In the same way, every good tree bears good fruit, but the bad tree bears bad fruit. A good tree cannot bear bad fruit, nor can a bad tree bear good fruit. Every tree that does not bear good fruit will be cut down and thrown into the fire. Thus you will know them by their fruits."

Yesterday, we looked at what Jesus might mean when he uses the metaphor of 'ravenous wolves'. We saw that, for a teacher to qualify as a 'ravenous wolf', there does not have to be any ulterior motive behind his/her teaching. It's just that his/her failure to understand Jesus' words makes him/her a destructive influence in the lives of everyone who follows him/her. Of course we would like to steer clear from such a teacher who would lead us to our destruction. Hence, Jesus tells us what to look out for.

Now, we saw the day before yesterday that, even

though Jesus seems to be addressing leaders, due to the thoroughly integrated nature of the Church, everyone is potentially a 'teacher' or 'prophet' and is, therefore, responsible under Jesus' words. 'True prophets' enable people to obey Jesus. They do not excuse people from the difficulties of discipleship by 'spiritualizing' Jesus' words. 'False prophets', on the other hand, teach people to disobey. Jesus is talking about people who do not enable others to enter through the narrow gate. These people, by their words and actions, recommend the easier path. For instance, they might excuse retaliatory behavior on grounds that "some people only understand the language of violence." On the other hand, they may openly applaud rich donors hoping to give other rich people the incentive of recognition. Alternatively, they might advocate hatred of a certain group of people based on the argument that "God hates such perverts." Once again, such people need not act out of impure motives. Rather, themselves on the path to destruction, having rejected the narrow path, they cannot but contribute to the destruction of others.

This allows us to see how dangerous discipleship to Jesus can be. Since in the Church our lives are enmeshed with each others' lives, if I am misguided, then I might have the best of intentions but would still mislead others.

Hence, Jesus asks us to pay attention to the fruit. He contrasts 'good fruit' and 'bad fruit'. 'Good fruit' obviously comes from a 'good tree' and 'bad fruit' from a 'bad tree'. In context and to mix metaphors somewhat, the 'good tree' is the one that is watered on the 'narrow road' while the 'bad tree' is the one that drinks from the 'wide road'.

Jesus has given us a few examples for what being nourished on the 'narrow road' would look like. It would look like being in control of one's anger, avoiding the 'second look', remaining faithful to one's marriage vows, speaking the truth without the need for oaths, not resorting to violence, loving one's enemies, not putting on a show of spirituality, having a forgiving disposition, treasuring the values of God's kingdom above everything else, having a generous disposition, rejecting coming into the service of money, trusting that God is good, refusing to worry because we trust God's goodness and faithfulness, refusing to condemn other people, judging ourselves with greater severity than we judge others, recognizing the right time for forgiveness that leads to restoration, praying with expectation and persistence, and acting out of empathy toward others. While it does not cover every aspect of our lives, Jesus has touched on many significant areas of life. And his teaching is clear if we do not allow ourselves to be blindsided by ideas that he is concerned about the sweet by and by!

So those who do not foster in others the behaviors Jesus promotes are false teachers, who lead people to their destruction. Since this is crucially important, I ask you, the reader, to honestly check if the Christians who wield some influence in your life are enabling you to prioritize the kinds of behaviors that Jesus promotes or if they are hindering you. If the former, praise God. If the latter, you have been duly warned.

Week 11, Day 4: Matthew 7.15-20

"Beware of false prophets, who come to you in sheep's clothing but inwardly are ravenous wolves. You will know them by their fruits. Are grapes gathered from thorns or figs from thistles? In the same way, every good tree bears good fruit, but the bad tree bears bad fruit. A good tree cannot bear bad fruit, nor can a bad tree bear good fruit. Every tree that does not bear good fruit will be cut down and thrown into the fire. Thus you will know them by their fruits."

In the previous three devotions, we have seen that those who are false prophets do not necessarily have bad intentions. A teacher with the best of intentions can lead people astray if he/she has misunderstood Jesus' words or who has understood and has chosen not to prioritize Jesus' words. But in these verses Jesus says, "Every tree that does not bear good fruit will be cut down and thrown into the fire."

Does this mean that a teacher like me has to be afraid because, if I teach something that is incorrect, I will be thrown into hell? Due to our conditioning to understand the language of cutting off and throwing into a fire as references to never ending punishment in hell, we are unable to appreciate what Jesus is saying. This is, in my opinion, a case of severe lack of theological imagination. Somehow, when it comes to the bible, we jettison all our ability to interpret things in a nuanced manner.

For example, almost all of us as children have faced different kinds of discipline from our parents. At times our parents placed a retributive model of discipline before us. At other times, their approach was restorative. Those of us who are parents can also recognize that we have not disciplined our children in uniform ways. There were times when we resorted to more punitive methods. At other times, we took a rehabilitative approach. I don't know about you, but I have found that the retributive or punitive approach works to produce quick results, but actually does not produce a change in character. On the other hand, the restorative or rehabilitative approach doesn't produce immediate results, but does tend to transform the child's character.

Now, place yourself in God's shoes. If we as human children and parents recognize that rehabilitation is better than punishment, restoration better than retribution, do we think

God does not know this? And if we who are parents, and weak, frail parents at that, are able to implement restorative and rehabilitative discipline with our children, do we think God's hands are tied, rendering him paralyzed when it comes to doing the same with us?

You see, when a tree or branch is cut off because it is fruitless, the tree or branch is *not* discarded. When it is thrown into the fire, it is actually being put to good use, as firewood, something that we city slickers cannot even understand. In other words, throwing something into the fire absolutely *does not* indicate consigning a person to never ending torment in hell. That is a view read into the text.

However, we also fail to recognize that fire has a dual role, both recognized in the bible. Fire can consume. And fire can purify. But actually both these roles function together. Fire purifies what cannot be consumed precisely because it consumes what can be consumed. In fact, when wood is burned, it serves as fuel. And the wood ash left behind is mineral rich and is often used in fertilizers, composts, pottery, soaps, paints, the food industry, and even to make beauty products.. In other words, even the residue left after burning is of great use.

What this tells us is that, if a person is found to be unfit as a teacher, he/she may be removed from such a position and placed in another position. This may happen before their death or after their death. What the image tells me is that there is always a reckoning for what I teach. If I teach something wrong intentionally, then there is an accounting for that. If I teach something wrong unintentionally, then there is a different kind of accounting for that. I may be removed from a sphere of influence before my death or after my death. But through the process of purification, all the wrong ideas will be burned away, leaving what can be used in the service of God's rule.

Week 11, Day 5: Matthew 7.15-20

"Beware of false prophets, who come to you in sheep's clothing but inwardly are ravenous wolves. You will know them by their fruits. Are grapes gathered from thorns or figs from thistles? In the same way, every good tree bears good fruit, but the bad tree bears bad fruit. A good tree cannot bear bad fruit, nor can a bad tree bear good fruit. Every tree that does not bear good fruit will be cut down and thrown into the fire. Thus you will know them by their fruits."

We know that an apple tree cannot become an orange tree and vice versa. Hence, when Jesus uses the language of 'good tree' and 'bad tree' we might be led to believe that this means that there are some people who are just rotten from the core and who cannot be rehabilitated, while there are other people who are wonderful souls who do not need rehabilitation. If we think this way, we are interpreting the metaphor of trees in a way that is at odds with what Jesus clearly teaches elsewhere.

You see, Jesus began his ministry with a call to repentance. If people are either 'good' or 'bad' then there actually is no hope of repentance. After all, a leopard cannot change its spots! In that case, Jesus' call to repentance is disingenuous because underlying any command, in this case 'repent', must be the idea that the command can be fulfilled. However, if people are either 'good' or 'bad', this means that the 'bad' people *cannot* fulfill the command because it is just not in their DNA.

I don't know about you, but I do not like the idea of Jesus being a disingenuous teacher. I believe that, when he issues a command, we are actually able, if not willing, to fulfill the command. Hence, since Jesus issues the command to repent, he must believe that *all* humans are capable of changing their minds about even the very important things.

So what is Jesus getting at by talking about 'good trees' and 'bad trees'? I take my cue from Matthew 16.23, where Jesus tells Peter, "Get behind me, Satan! You are a hindrance to me, for you are setting your mind not on divine things but on human things." Now, none of us thinks that Peter should be identified with Satan. Nor do we think that, whatever link Jesus is drawing between Peter and Satan, such a link is permanent. To the contrary, *at that moment* Peter was functioning like Satan, Jesus' primary adversary.

In the same way, a 'good tree' is one that is producing 'good fruit' *at that moment*, while a 'bad tree' is one that is producing 'bad fruit' *at that moment*. What this means is that everyone who teaches functions like a 'good tree' at times and like a 'bad tree' at other times. Some may have a better streak at being 'good trees' and we should align ourselves with such teachers. Others may have a track record of being 'bad trees' and we should attempt to distance ourselves from such teachers.

In other words, rather than place us in predetermined and unalterable categories, Jesus tells anyone who presumes to teach that he/she should be vigilant about what he/she teaches. If I have a track record of being a 'good tree' that does not exclude me from the possibility of being a 'bad tree' on some future occasion. Similarly, just because I have a track record as a 'bad tree' this does not mean I cannot repent and become a 'good tree' in the future.

Jesus' words, as always, ask us to constantly check ourselves. Prior faithfulness should lead to hope, but not overconfidence. Similarly, former failures should not lead to despair, but should empower us to once again connect ourselves to Jesus' teachings. Indeed, as we proceed to the last segment of the Sermon on the Mount, we will see that this is just what Jesus encourages us to do.

"Not everyone who says to me, 'Lord, Lord,' will enter the kingdom of heaven, but only the one who does the will of my Father in heaven. On that day many will say to me, 'Lord, Lord, did we not prophesy in your name, and cast out demons in your name, and do many mighty works in your name?' Then I will declare to them, 'I never knew you; go away from me, you who behave lawlessly.'"

In earlier sessions, we observed that the "false prophets" are indistinguishable from other Christians on confessional and ministerial grounds. That is, "false prophets" address Jesus as Lord and perform mighty deeds in his name. In fact, they do believe Jesus is Lord and become vehicles of miracles because of that belief. The reason for which they receive harsh words from Jesus is that they did not do the will of God. We need to keep in mind that Jesus is not teaching salvation by works. Neither, when he says, "I have never known you," does he mean that the people he rebukes were never Christian. Rather, his words are designed to underscore the immense importance of obeying him. The people are chastised because they disobeyed.

If Jesus is so serious about our doing God's will, how easy is it to know God's mind? After all, we can deliberately do what God desires only if we are privy to what he would have us do. We must observe that Jesus does not have specific circumstances in mind. What he has in mind are the contents of the Sermon on the Mount. For instance, after hearing him say, "Blessed are the merciful," we disobey him if we do not attempt to be merciful. Similarly, after hearing him tell us, "Love your enemies," we disobey him if we find excuses for hating our enemies.

In other words, Jesus says, "I have never known you" to Christians who ignore what he says in the Sermon on the Mount and who find reasons for rejecting his teachings. These reasons are so innocuous that we need to mention a few of them. One argument goes: Jesus is describing the Messianic age; he does not expect obedience now. Another thesis runs like this: The Sermon describes impossible discipleship; Jesus does that so we can come to him to receive grace, not so that we obey him. A third proposal is this: Jesus is God; only he can fulfill the Sermon; we mere humans cannot obey his teachings; he obeys his own Sermon for us.

All these excuses for disobedience are contrary to Jesus' clear intent in the Sermon. Indeed, his words in today's verses would mean nothing if he did not mean them with all sincerity. Jesus places obedience to him above belief. After all, belief without obedience is dead. When Jesus says, "I have never known you," he is giving voice to his utter rejection of all our cop-out ways of reasoning. Just as we might say, "I don't know who you are" to someone we have known for years, but who surprises us by doing something out of character, so also Jesus says, "I have never known you" to Christians who reject his teachings in the Sermon. What Jesus is saying is that seeking ways to justify disobedience to the Sermon is out of character for a Christian. Therefore, we should see in Jesus' words "I have never known you," a potent expression of bewilderment at the behavior of people—in this case Christians—who should have known better. We will address this at greater length later.

Given Jesus' charge that we should be willing to forgive without count, it would seem strange if he were not going to model that kind of behavior for us. Hence, it would seem that this is a dismissal of people who had rejected his teachings with the specific purpose that they would learn not to reject those teachings anymore. In other words, rather than being a punitive dismissal, this is, in my view, a pedagogical dismissal through which Jesus gives the person another chance to realize how wholesome his way of living is. We will look at this in greater detail later.

Week 11, Day 7: Matthew 7.21-23

"Not everyone who says to me, 'Lord, Lord,' will enter the kingdom of heaven, but only the one who does the will of my Father in heaven. On that day many will say to me, 'Lord, Lord, did we not prophesy in your name, and cast out demons in your name, and do many mighty works in your name?' Then I will declare to them, 'I never knew you; go away from me, you who behave lawlessly.'"

Over the course of my time as a disciple of Jesus, I have heard many other Christians point to this or that prominent Christian teacher and say that he/she has such a great ministry and that we should look up to such people and aspire to have ministries like them. However, I am sure that most of us are aware that many Christian leaders have been exposed for various crimes and moral failures. Not all, of course. There are many who have been people of strong character. However, the fact that there have been not just a few but a large number of Christian leaders who have demonstrated poor character and moral turpitude should serve as a warning to us.

Now, it is possible that some of these people, who have been exposed in the past, started their work with the ulterior motive of stealing from others or of dominating others. However, I am confident that most of them started with the best of intentions and expected to benefit and serve the people they ministered to. However, the lack of oversight from any external body (e.g. the government) and the lack of incentive from inside the church or Christian organization to expose their own leaders makes churches and Christian organizations fertile grounds for the development and nurturing of exploitative and toxic leaders, who, in the end, only serve themselves and not the people they purport to serve.

Note that Jesus does not deny the work they did. As Joseph told his brothers, it is possible for God to bring good out of the most evil of intentions. That is, even though his brothers sold him into slavery, God was able to bring good from that horrible circumstance. Hence, even if Christian leaders are exploitative and toxic, God is able to benefit many through them. What this means is that the benefits that flow from any person's ministry to others should not be seen as a way of measuring whether that person is being faithful to Jesus or not. It is possible that the benefits are flowing *despite* the exploitative and toxic ways of the leader rather than *because of* them.

However, it is crucial to observe that this does not mean that these exploitative and toxic leaders do not have a relationship with Jesus. They tell Jesus that they did all those great things "in your name." This does not mean that they used the name of Jesus in their prayers and incantations or whatever other formulas they used in their ministries. Why do I say this?

Well, for one, the son of Mary, whom we call Lord and whose sermon we are studying, was never called 'Jesus'. 'Jesus' is an anglicized form of his name and not his real name. His mother probably called him 'Yehoshua' or 'Yeshua'. If it is true that the name *per se* is what gives a leader authority, then the whole of the Christian Church from the first document written has been floundering with the wrong name. After all, in Galatians 1.1 itself, Paul begins with the words, "Paul an apostle—sent neither by human commission nor from human authorities but through Jesus Christ and God the Father, who raised him from the dead," where, for 'Jesus', the Greek text reads 'Iésous', which is certainly not what Mary called him.

The phrase 'in the name of Jesus' refers not to Jesus' name but to the authority of Jesus. When I say that I am doing something "in the name of Jesus" it means that I am invoking Jesus' authority for the task I am undertaking. This would be an empty claim if I did not have Jesus' permission to use his name in this way. The sons of Sceva discovered this in Acts 19.11 when they tried to invoke the authority of Jesus on the basis of the relationship Paul had with Jesus. Since they had no relationship with Jesus, the evil spirits overpowered them.

Since the leaders are able to claim that they did their mighty works in Jesus' name, it means that they had a relationship with him. This is all the more devastating because it shows us that it is possible for us to have a relationship with Jesus and still abuse that relationship in ways that harm others.

Week 12

Week 12, Day 1: Matthew 7.21-23

"Not everyone who says to me, 'Lord, Lord,' will enter the kingdom of heaven, but only the one who does the will of my Father in heaven. On that day many will say to me, 'Lord, Lord, did we not prophesy in your name, and cast out demons in your name, and do many mighty works in your name?' Then I will declare to them, 'I never knew you; go away from me, you who behave lawlessly.'"

Yesterday, I claimed that the fact that the people Jesus chastises here were able to do mighty works in his name was that they had a relationship with him. Yet, Jesus tells them, "I never knew you." What does he mean? In order to understand Jesus, we need to allow him the full use of language and not box him in as though he was only able to speak in monotones and in a serious, ponderous manner.

I'm sure most of us have had a close friend who

surprised us with something he said or something she did. Those words or actions would have come from out of the blue as far as we were concerned. In response, we might have said something like, "I don't even know who you are!" And we would use these words only if our friend had disappointed us with his words or her actions. But note that these words do not mean that we never had a relationship with them. Rather, and ironically, these words imply a very close and intimate relationship that has now been denied by the words and actions of the friend.

Hence, when Jesus tells the person, "I never knew you," he is actually saying that there is a deep relationship between him and the person but that the person had denied the relationship. Of course, with the denial of the relationship, the parties (i.e. Jesus and the person) cannot continue as though nothing had happened. The person had denied his/her relationship with Jesus by failing to speak and act in ways that reflected Jesus' character. If Jesus simply allowed that person to continue as is, he would be denying his own character by saying that the person's denial was no big deal. However, we cannot have a new creation in which even one person is not fully conformed to the image of God's Son. Hence, the person needs to be reformed.

To this end, Jesus sends the person away. When he says, "Go away from me," it is crucial to note that he does not add the word 'forever'. The going away is not to be construed as a permanent state of affairs. Rather, the bible shows us many cases in which a banishment or exile is used by God for the specific purpose of instructing those who are banished or exiled. We can think of Adam and Eve, of Cain, of Jonah, and, of course, the exile – the quintessential 'going away' event of the Old Testament that was specifically intended to teach the people of Israel that faithfulness to Yahweh was non-negotiable.

On account of this, any view that takes Jesus' words, "Go away from me," as indicating a permanent situation betrays a complete failure to understand the role of banishment and exile in the biblical narrative. God certainly disciplines us. But he does this because he wants us to have the best character we can have. And we will when our characters are completely aligned with the character of Jesus. However, God's discipline is never punitive or retributive but always palliative and restorative.

"Everyone, then, who hears these words of mine and acts on them will be like a wise man who built his house on rock. The rain fell, the floods came, and the winds blew and beat on that house, but it did not fall because it had been founded on rock. And everyone who hears these words of mine and does not act on them will be like a foolish man who built his house on sand. The rain fell, and the floods came, and the winds blew and beat against that house, and it fell—and great was its fall!"

This is a well-known, but very often misused or misinterpreted, part of the Sermon on the Mount. Many people who grew up in the church will have sung some songs in Sunday School about a wise man who built his house upon the rock. However, when the song conveniently avoids telling us what classifies the wise man as a wise man, singing it does not prove to be a transformative experience.

Jesus begins by saying that anyone who hears his words and acts on them is like a wise man/woman, who builds on a rock. In contrast, anyone who hears his words and does not act on them is like a foolish man/woman, who builds on sand. Jesus is so clear that I wonder how the Church has, for the most part, managed to miss what he says.

For Jesus' simile to work, 'rock' and 'sand' must be parallel with 'acts on it' and 'does not act on it'. In other words, Jesus is not the rock here! Nor is orthodox belief the rock. Rather, the rock is a person's adherence to Jesus' words. The rock that provides security and stability through life's vicissitudes is a person's obedience to Jesus. If I obey Jesus, I will find that this obedience grants me security and stability to deal with all challenges I may face. However, if I disobey Jesus, then *even if I have the most orthodox beliefs*, I will find that I will not be able to face the challenges of life.

Given that we have been conditioned for centuries *against* Jesus' clear teaching here, it pays to remind ourselves that, when Jesus speaks of a house that was founded on the rock, he *does not* mean that he is the rock. In this context *Jesus is not the rock!* Nor is he saying, as some Protestant interpretations of Matthew 16.18 erroneously claim, that the rock is the confession that Jesus is the Messiah, the Son of the living God.

Rather, he could not be clearer in claiming that obedience to his words is the rock on which we will find the stability and security needed to weather all the storms life brings our way.

The only reason I can think why many Christians do not see this is because they have elevated the rejection of what they call 'works righteousness' as the supreme endeavor of the Christian faith. According to them, we must never even appear as though we say that something we do is actually crucial for a Christian. And so great is their aversion to this 'works righteousness' that they are even willing to misread Jesus' words in order to support their position. However, a careful reading of Jesus' words and the parallels he draws through his similes will indicate that Jesus expects obedience as the rock on which people must build.

The problem is threefold. First, people erroneously think that Jesus is talking about 'salvation', as though he had nothing else on his mind. As maintained in previous devotions, Jesus is supremely concerned with how we act here and now. If we say that he wasn't concerned about how we act here and now, we might as well jettison the whole of the Sermon on the Mount, because every part of it is about how we behave here and now. Of course, there have been Christian teachers who have jettisoned the Sermon on the Mount as irrelevant for us today. There have been others, who, correctly understanding Jesus' insistence on obedience, advocate a doctrine known as 'lordship salvation'. However, if this passage is not about 'salvation' then this passage cannot be used to support such a doctrine.

Second, as we have seen, all language about 'cutting down' or 'throwing in a fire' and, in this passage, 'falling down' is understood as a never ending punishment, a state from which one cannot recover, and a state in which one is being punished for all one's failures. However, as we have seen, discipline *does not* need to be retributive and punitive. It is possible for all discipline to be rehabilitative and restorative.

Third, there is a tendency to not appreciate consequences as divine judgment. Just as a house with a weak foundation will be wrecked in a storm precisely because of its weak foundation, so also a person who does not obey Jesus will find his/her life in shambles when faced with difficulties. This is not a punishment on the part of God. Rather, it is just what happens to a life that is not built on a foundation that could withstand the challenges of life. If we are designed to operate in alignment with Jesus' teachings, then it should come as no surprise if we find ourselves unraveling when we decide not to align ourselves with his teachings.

"Everyone, then, who hears these words of mine and acts on them will be like a wise man who built his house on rock. The rain fell, the floods came, and the winds blew and beat on that house, but it did not fall because it had been founded on rock. And everyone who hears these words of mine and does not act on them will be like a foolish man who built his house on sand. The rain fell, and the floods came, and the winds blew and beat against that house, and it fell—and great was its fall!"

While we saw yesterday that Jesus is drawing a parallel between acting on his words and building on a rock, some interpreters have seen a more polemic side to his words.

In the Jewish imagination, the 'house' that was 'built on a rock' was quintessentially the temple. It was built on what is today called the Temple Mount or the Dome of the Rock, which is referred to as the 'mount of the house' in Micah 4.1 and Jeremiah 26.18.

According to this view, Jesus is explicitly contrasting

adherence to the temple practices with obedience to him. Toward the start of the Sermon on the Mount, Jesus had said, "Do not think that I have come to abolish the Law or the Prophets; I have come not to abolish but to fulfill." Of course, right after that he proceeds to issue teaching on a variety of issues. And his teaching is often in tension with what is taught in the Old Testament. We could certainly claim that he is not actually opposing anything in the Old Testament, but is making the Old Testament stricter. Such a claim can easily be supported by comparing the relevant passages in the Old Testament with those parts of the Sermon.

However, we need to be honest here. Suppose the sentence for some crime is imprisonment for five years. Suppose, however, a judge sentences a person found guilty of that crime to six years' imprisonment. We could say that the judge is making the law stricter. But more appropriate would be to say that the judge is actually violating the law. I'm sure the poor person, who was sentenced to six years rather than five years, would claim violation of the law!

Hence, even if Jesus makes the Torah stricter and in so doing does not abolish the Torah, we must admit that he creates a tension between his teachings and the Torah.

Now the temple was the center of Torah observance. It was where violations of Torah observance could be adjudicated. In other words, one of the purposes of the temple was to monitor and support observance of the Torah.

When Jesus issues his teaching and in so doing introduces a tension between his words and what is practiced in the temple, he also issues a challenge to those who have heard his teaching. Do they obey him or continue to submit themselves to the teachings that were monitored and supported by the temple? This is no trivial decision for a Jew. And we dare not forget that *all* of Jesus' first disciples were Jews.

Jesus was explicitly stating that obedience to his teachings is a replacement to whatever the temple provided. By extension, he was saying the unthinkable, namely that obedience to the temple was not a way of building on a rock, but was actually building on sand. Those who, after hearing his words, continued to submit themselves to the teaching of the temple were duping themselves and were actually building on sand. And this would result in their unraveling when they were faced with the storms that lay ahead.

It is likely that Jesus had in mind the tendency of the Jewish people to launch messianic revolts against their occupiers. Drawing from the conquest narratives in Joshua and Judges, Jews who adopted violent tactics easily found support for their actions against the occupiers. Jesus would later indicate that such violent actions would actually result in the destruction of Jerusalem and the temple. With his imagery about a deluge that pulls a house down because it is built on sand, he is likely declaring, in a very symbolic and, at this moment in Matthew, opaque manner, that obedience to the temple will cause its own destruction.

"Everyone, then, who hears these words of mine and acts on them will be like a wise man who built his house on rock. The rain fell, the floods came, and the winds blew and beat on that house, but it did not fall because it had been founded on rock. And everyone who hears these words of mine and does not act on them will be like a foolish man who built his house on sand. The rain fell, and the floods came, and the winds blew and beat against that house, and it fell—and great was its fall!"

One thing that never struck me in earlier years but came to me only quite recently is that Jesus does not narrate this parable with any doubt concerning whether or not the rains would fall. Of course, the rains in this parable represent the difficulties that we face in our lives. What Jesus seems to be indicating is that everyone will face times of extreme crises.

Now, what is a crisis to one person may seem like smooth sailing to another. As the popular illustration goes, boiling water makes a hard potato soft and a soft egg hard. The common lesson drawn from this is, "What you are on the inside determines how you respond to adversity." But the illustration fails because no one in their right mind wants to eat a hard potato. And though I myself care very little for hard-boiled eggs, those who boil the egg long enough, probably want it hard! What I am trying to say is that we should not compare our trials with those of others. Adversity is not a matter of weighing on a beam balance to determine who 'wins' by having more of it. Rather, adversity is a matter of character development. And if one person needs to be softened while another hardened, then the adversity that each person faces is well able to accomplish the transformation.

However, we need to ask ourselves what the 'fall' Jesus mentions in these verses might be. Unfortunately, there is a tendency within the church to think of damnation and the eternal fires of hell whenever Jesus (or anyone else in the bible for that matter) speaks of judgment or issues a warning. Yet, just before he unveils the prospect of a new covenant, God announces through Jeremiah, "And just as I have watched over them to pluck up and break down, to overthrow, destroy, and bring evil, so I will watch over them to build and to plant, says the Lord." (Jeremiah 31.28) In other words, the plucking up and breaking down of the people of Israel, brought to life in the exile, were only preludes to the building up and planting.

Now, the exile is clearly portrayed as God's judgment on the people of Israel for their failure to form a just society. Hence, if there is building up and planting at the end of even a harsh judgment like the exile, we should expect no less for all the adversities we may face. That is, even though we are facing the most difficult of situations, God's eventual purpose for us is *always* restoration.

In light of this, what could the 'fall' that Jesus refers to represent? In order to answer this, we must first decide what the 'house' is. This is something we 'build', something we construct. What could this be?

I think it is best to think of this as our sense of identity. If we build our sense of identity on the foundation of obedience to Jesus' teachings, then that sense of identity will be in alignment with God's purposes for us. In such a case, we will be able to withstand all the adversities that may come our way. However, any identity that is built without being founded on obedience to Jesus' teachings is an identity that is not reflective of the purpose for which God has created us. Hence, when adversities come our way, that sense of identity is toppled and called into question.

At the same time, given the fact that God's judgment is always followed by restoration, the toppling of our false sense of identity is not the end. Rather, the destruction of the false sense of identity itself produces the space within which a new identity built on Jesus' teachings can begin.

Week 12, Day 5: The Beatitudes

Blessed are the poor in spirit, for theirs is the kingdom of heaven. Blessed are those who mourn, for they will be comforted. Blessed are the meek, for they will inherit the earth. Blessed are those who hunger and thirst for righteousness, for they will be filled. Blessed are the merciful, for they will receive mercy. Blessed are the pure in heart, for they will see God. Blessed are the peacemakers, for they will be called children of God. Blessed are those who are persecuted for the sake of righteousness, for theirs is the kingdom of heaven. Blessed are you when people revile you and persecute you and utter all kinds of evil against you falsely on my account. Rejoice and be glad, for your reward is great in heaven, for in the same way they persecuted the prophets who were before you.

The Sermon on the Mount begins with eight brief statements about the kind of people who are blessed, followed by a lengthier summary blessing addressed in second person. As we saw, there is somewhat of an 'intensification' as we proceed

331

from the first beatitude to the eighth, with the ninth probably functioning as a catch all blessing to indicate what we can expect if the traits described by the beatitudes start transforming us.

Often we think of Jesus' teachings in the Sermon on the Mount as being so hard that they are impossible to fulfill. This leads to the conclusion that Jesus' intention is to drive us to despair so we may understand our inability. Then we are in a position to accept the grace that Jesus offers. However, such a line of thinking portrays Jesus as someone who rubs our noses in the dirt just so he can then clean us. Such thinking also gives us an excuse for not trying to follow Jesus. And frankly, any line of thought that makes Jesus the excuse for not attempting to follow him is flawed and should be avoided.

Jesus is painting, with the colors of the beatitudes, a picture of those who belong to God's kingdom. They show their citizenship by the ethos or traits they replicate. They avoid evaluating the spiritual condition of others. They mourn with others. They seek the welfare of others above their own welfare. They seek to relate rightly with others. And they choose to be disadvantaged. For sure, these traits are not our natural inclination. And these traits are often looked down upon by other people. However, these are not traits that are beyond us—not if we are truly Jesus' disciples. We can refrain from spiritual evaluation. We can mourn instead of pushing sorrow under the rug and "getting on with life." We can refuse to play by the rules of one-upmanship. We can relate correctly with others. And we can show mercy. The strange thing is that the more we practice these qualities, the more we will realize both that we need God and that with God we can become the kind of people Jesus depicts in the beatitudes. The paradox is that the more we resist following Jesus, the more difficult it is to follow him; the more we submit to his teachings, the more grace we are able to receive.

It also pays to remind ourselves that these are not qualifying traits of some kind, nor ways in which we demonstrate some kind of spiritual superiority over others. That itself would go against the grain of the beatitudes, which start with the blessing on those who are impoverished. Rather, these are traits that humans do not often value. Our societies do not place much emphasis on developing these traits.

However, these are the kinds of traits that allow us a glimpse into the heart of God. Actually, these are the only traits that can be universalized and produce a world in which every person is enabled to flourish and thrive. A world composed of people defined by the traits described in the beatitudes is a world that is self-sustaining and one that can build on the past to stabilize the present and provide hope for the future.

Unfortunately, it is easy to entertain the notion that Jesus is speaking about our private devotional life—that we should be pure and undefiled and have peace of mind or peaceful dispositions. Even his words about persecution we reduce to the individual level of our feeling hurt when people ridicule us for avoiding immoral behavior. Jesus does speak of our private lives—but not here!

Here he is describing a community of reconcilers, wholly dedicated to bringing God's mercy and faithfulness, grace and truth, to bear on the lives of everyone on earth. Probably because the task is so enormous, we find it easy to water down Jesus' words and to apply them to our personal devotion. But do we see the arrogance involved in that? When Jesus is describing what we should be for a broken world, we make him out to be describing what we should be in and for ourselves!

It is no wonder then that we often find Jesus' words

burdensome. We strive to be pure, only to find ourselves impure at every juncture. We work at having peace of mind, only to be ravaged by discontent and cravings. We add up spiritual brownie points every time someone ridicules us for some "righteous" behavior, only to be hounded by the realization that God does not hand out brownie points. Why? Why have Jesus' words become burdensome? It is because we try to use them in a manner for which they were not designed.

In much of Matthew's Gospel Jesus finds fault with the Pharisees and scribes, not because they strove for personal purity and piety, but because they neglected the relational aspects of mercy and faithfulness, grace and truth. Could it be that, if Jesus were around today, he would speak of our neglect of "the weightier matters of the Law—justice, mercy, faith" (Matthew 23.23)?

The beatitudes are inherently relational, as we saw earlier. And if these are the colors with which Jesus chose to paint a picture of those who belong to God's kingdom, then we cannot but come away with the conclusion that, to belong to God's kingdom is to be involved in deep relationships with other humans.

It is time to rid ourselves of the pernicious influence that individualism has had on the life and witness of the Church. It is time once again to embrace the communal living that ought to characterize the Church of Jesus. For too long we have lionized supposedly towering figures of faith as though they had no community behind them, supporting them and enabling them to accomplish what they did. It is time to 'lambize' ourselves into a community in which service is elevated as the way of leading and in which mutual contributions of everyone is recognized and valued.

The problem is that we cannot systematize this, as Church history amply illustrates. As soon as we lay down some set of 'criteria' that we value, we will undermine the very idea behind those criteria. It must always remain something that is *ad hoc* rather than defined. That is the only way we can free ourselves from the trap that Jesus later addresses - that of putting on a show for others to applaud.

Week 12, Day 6: Salt and Light

You are the salt of the earth, but if salt has lost its taste, how can its saltiness be restored? It is no longer good for anything but is thrown out and trampled under foot. You are the light of the world. A city built on a hill cannot be hid. 15 People do not light a lamp and put it under the bushel basket; rather, they put it on the lampstand, and it gives light to all in the house. In the same way, let your light shine before others, so that they may see your good works and give glory to your Father in heaven.

Salt and light are so essential, so common that we could easily fail to see what Jesus is getting at through the two metaphors. The idea of our being salt wars against our tendency toward triumphalism for salt works best when it is a minority and unseen. At the same time the notion of our being light battles our false humility, which often is only a façade covering our fear or indecisiveness. Allowing the two metaphors to play off each other, we could say that we are meant to be a visible minority—a minority whose visible deeds are so potent as to pierce into the fortresses of darkness in the world.

We could also say that salt is a subversive metaphor since salt works unseen without changing the external appearance of the thing upon which it is acting. However, light is not at all subversive. It works openly, dispelling the darkness but shedding light on all who were formerly shrouded in the darkness. Both metaphors point to our being agents of change in the world. However, we require God's wisdom to decide when it is best to effect change openly and when subversive means are needed.

Both metaphors are 'peaceful' metaphors. Light casts out darkness but does not harm those formerly entombed in darkness. Salt infiltrates the substance in order to preserve, to bring out flavor, or to sterilize wounds. Both metaphors warn against using harmful tactics in our discipleship. Oppression, deception, malice, vengeance, violence, corruption, pride, selfishness, etc. are all contrary to what Jesus says. That the church has not been careful in this regard might indicate a reason for which the gospel is so easily rejected in the most well-reached areas of the world.

In fact, the most well-reached areas of the world, unfortunately, considered the forming of 'Christian' nations as a mandate from God. But in so doing they surrendered the nonviolence of the gospel for a twisted message based on state sponsored violence. However, when Jesus tells Pilate that his kingdom is not from this world, he specifically links it to a violent attempt to liberate him. Granted that he had been captured on false pretenses, his capture was illegal. Hence, his liberation should have been a no brainer. In fact, if ever there was a case where we could have found justification for the use of violence to rectify some wrong, it would have been the case of Jesus' capture. Yet, even in this case, Jesus is clear that his disciples would not resort to violence precisely because his kingdom is not aligned with this world's definitions of 'kingdom'.

Yet, so steeped are we in the mentality arising from the idea of a 'Christian' nation that we Christians go to great extents to justify the violence perpetrated by our nations in our names. It is time to recover the metaphors of 'salt' and 'light' in all their nonviolent potency. It is time to recover the understanding that Jesus *does not* gain his victory in the way the nations of this world do. He does not press his case at the tip of a sword. Rather, he attempts to persuade through his Church, which is supposed to be 'salt' and 'light' in a world that is enslaved to violence.

Week 12, Day 7: Jesus and *Torah*

Do not think that I have come to abolish the Law or the Prophets; I have come not to abolish but to fulfill. For truly I tell you, until heaven and earth pass away, not one letter, not one stroke of a letter, will pass from the law until all is accomplished. Therefore, whoever breaks one of the least of these commandments and teaches others to do the same will be called least in the kingdom of heaven, but whoever does them and teaches them will be called great in the kingdom of heaven. For I tell you, unless your righteousness exceeds that of the scribes and Pharisees, you will never enter the kingdom of heaven.

Probably the most unfortunate translation is that of the word *nomos*. While *nomos* means 'law', this was the Greek word used to translate the Hebrew word *torah*. Unfortunately, the early Church, with its dependence on Greek and scholars of Greek, often forgot that the New Testament was written mostly by first century Jews. It is likely that only Luke and Acts are written by a non-Jewish person. The early Church fathers, however, failed to appreciate that Jewish writers would have had Jewish ideas behind their words *even when* they were writing in Greek. Hence, they assumed Greek meanings of *nomos* rather than Hebrew meanings of *torah* to underlie the New Testament usage of the Greek word *nomos*.

However, to be faithful to an author, we must ask ourselves what that author might have been thinking of when he used a certain word. And it is clear to me that a Jewish author would have had Hebraic ideas behind his words rather than Greco-Roman ideas. While *torah* means instruction or teaching, most English translations render *nomos* with 'law'. This has us thinking of our relationship with God as being like that between a subject and a dictator. Then we think of God rewarding or punishing us based on our obedience or disobedience. How can we love someone truly if we think that he has defined his relationship with us along these lines? It is no wonder, then, that our songs of love to God lack the real raw emotive passion that newlyweds have!

But what if *torah* is God's instruction for how we best do what we were created to do—that is, love him? Maybe by giving the Jews Torah God was saying, "I am madly in love with you. And I made you and chose you to be madly in love with me so that the others whom I have also made will be madly in love with me as I am with them. And here is the kind of life that will enable you to be passionate about me." Such an approach to *torah* frees us from adhering to it legalistically and woodenly. We can then apply it creatively to our specific contexts.

An example from the bible might help. In John 8, Jesus is faced with a quandary. Before him was a woman caught in adultery. *Torah* said that she should be stoned. Her accusers approached *torah* as a law set in stone and wanted Jesus to pronounce sentence on her. Jesus, however, approached *torah* as a whole set of instructions, which, if followed, would please God and enable passion for him. His reply accomplished two things. First, it told the accusers that the real purpose of *torah* was not so people could find fault with each other. Second, it showed the woman that God loved her and wanted her to experience it. In fact, God so greatly wanted her to experience his love that he was willing to set aside the 'requirement' of *torah* so she could 'sin no more' and learn how to return God's love.

We can see Jesus taking this approach with the Sabbath, with dietary restrictions, in situations that rendered people ritually unclean, etc. His bottom line was, "The Sabbath was made for humans, not humans for the Sabbath." In other words, Jesus is telling us that God's primary concern is for his human creatures. And if adherence to some aspect of *torah* reduced the ability of a human to thrive and flourish, then perhaps it was better to set that aspect aside for this particular situation.

Week 13

Week 13, Day 1: Anger, murder, lust, and adultery

You have heard that it was said to those of ancient times, 'You shall not murder,' and 'whoever murders shall be liable to judgment.' But I say to you that if you are angry with a brother or sister, you will be liable to judgment, and if you insult a brother or sister, you will be liable to the council, and if you say, 'You fool,' you will be liable to the hell of fire... You have heard that it was said, 'You shall not commit adultery.' But I say to you that everyone who looks at a woman with lust has already committed adultery with her in his heart. (Matthew 5.21-22, 27-29)

While most of us can claim to be non-murderers and non-adulterers, few of us—if any—can claim never to have said a spiteful word or never to have desired another person in an inappropriate manner. And it is quite possible that those who quickly claim exemptions even from these 'milder' sins would, after reflection, realize that they are not exempted. We have killed and sexually violated with our thoughts and words. We have treated others in inhumane ways.

But Jesus intends for us to have wholesome relationships in which we value and respect each other. He would have us relate to others in a manner that invests them with dignity and that recognizes their full humanity. This restoration of dignity is key to understanding Jesus' words and ministry. However, unlike popular psychology that argues for dignity apart from relationships, Jesus insists that dignity is inherently relational. We cannot be fully human without having wholesome relationships.

At the same time, we must remember that we live in a broken world and that we are broken people. Our relationships are broken. Therefore, while we take Jesus' words with utmost seriousness, we should not take them legalistically as though he is dictating a new law book. We should make every attempt to follow him, while being open to receiving his forgiveness when we disobey. After all, if relationships are so important to him, we should relate to him in an appropriate manner. And in relating to him, our primary posture must be one of receiving forgiveness!

And we can be sure that forgiveness is something he readily offers us. But forgiveness is not absolution from responsibility. Rather, forgiveness means that he does not hold our past against us. He does not use our past failings as reasons for breaking off a relationship with us. Indeed, forgiveness means a restoration of the relationship so that the future is not damaged by being held captive to the past.

When we looked at the way Jesus approached *torah*, we saw that he did not use *torah* as a way of condemning people. Rather, the way in which he used *torah* enabled people to understand how they had hurt others. This allowed them to repent and align their lives with the values of his kingdom. Condemnation would have been the end of the road, with no possibility of restoring the relationship. However, through forgiveness, we are enabled to continue with a relationship, while accepting responsibility for our past failings.

This means that we should not treat Jesus' words in a legalistic manner. He is not laying down a 'new law' for us to follow. Rather, through his words, he is opening our eyes to recognize where sin takes root in our lives and how it matures into full blown actions that violate the dignity and personhood of others. His words direct us to be vigilant about our thoughts and even some quite unconscious actions like the 'second look'. There is always grace for those who fail, because God is a God who forgives us. But this does not mean that we should not take seriously how we live.

Week 13, Day 2: Unmasking oppression

You have heard that it was said, 'An eye for an eye and a tooth for a tooth.' But I say to you: Do not resist an evildoer. But if anyone strikes you on the right cheek, turn the other also, and if anyone wants to sue you and take your shirt, give your coat as well, and if anyone forces you to go one mile, go also the second mile. Give to the one who asks of you, and do not refuse anyone who wants to borrow from you.

In these short verses, Jesus gives us a glimpse into the kinds of action he would encourage his disciples to take. In a world governed by systems of retaliatory 'justice' signified by the words, 'eye for an eye and tooth for a tooth', Jesus suggests a different approach. He briefly describes three situations which his audience would have been familiar with. In all three instances, he suggests acting without violent retaliation. However, he does not tell his disciples to be doormats, as is often understood.

Rather, in each of the three cases, Jesus shows his disciples how they can respond in a way that would unmask the existing structures of oppression through which people exploit each other. The actions he suggests enables his disciples to reclaim their dignity by not being people who are acted upon, but as people who take the initiative to break the cycles of oppression that, ironically, even enslave the oppressor.

What these verses provide us with are 'action templates' that allow us to see what ways of acting Jesus approves of. He could obviously have not covered the whole gamut of experience even for the Jews of his day, let alone address circumstances we face today. However, we can see that he presents to us a 'third way', one that neither responds with the oppressor's own methods, nor responds with an acceptance of the oppression.

Jesus seems to have considered some common forms of injustice in his day and mulled over these situations to arrive at possible nonviolent responses that would suitably challenge and expose oppression while reasserting the dignity of the oppressed person. His creativity is revealed when we consider that we would face none of these situations today because they are rooted in the experience of first century Palestinian Jews. This reveals to us that there are no universal responses. Rather, all responses are context specific. If we are to imitate Jesus, we need to do the difficult task of identifying oppressive situations, reflect on them, and come away with possible responses.

This calls for the use of imagination and intuition. If we are honest, we will admit that the responses Jesus suggests do not conform with what we might consider to be 'rational'. Turning the other cheek, giving our last item of clothing, carrying a load an extra mile are not things that we could have reasoned ourselves into. Rather, they work contrary to our common expectations. What this means is that the responses we may have to come up with in oppressive situations we face may not stare us in the face. We may have to wrestle with the situation to arrive at some course of action that would boggle the mind and seem 'unreasonable'.

Week 13, Day 3: Loving enemies

You have heard that it was said, 'You shall love your neighbor and hate your enemy.' But I say to you: Love your enemies and pray for those who persecute you, so that you may be children of your Father in heaven, for he makes his sun rise on the evil and on the good and sends rain on the righteous and on the unrighteous. For if you love those who love you, what reward do you have? Do not even the tax collectors do the same? And if you greet only your brothers and sisters, what more are you doing than others? Do not even the gentiles do the same? Be perfect, therefore, as your heavenly Father is perfect. (Matthew 5.43-48)

Jesus' call to discipleship is both urgent and radical. By 'radical' I do not mean some form of violent extremism. Rather, by 'radical' I mean something that addresses 'root causes'. In these verses Jesus identifies the reason for which our societies are broken and fragmented. And he advocates an approach toward other people that will ensure the healing of the world.

He tells us that what distinguishes those who follow

him and those who do not is the attitude of love for one's enemies. He tells us that, contrary to most religious ideas and, unfortunately, most of what passes off as 'Christian', God does not show favoritism. He blesses *all* his human creatures with all the essential blessings, like sunshine and rain, without which we could not exist.

While the bible is chock-full of the notion that God has a 'people' whom he calls his own, the bible is also clear that God does not bless his people so that they can hoard all the blessings. Rather, his people are set apart precisely for the task of being channels of blessings for others.

When Jesus asks us to love our enemies, he is saying precisely this. Just as God does not only bless those who are his 'friends', so also we must love even those who consider us their enemies. This is not an easy task since most of us are driven by a *quid pro quo* mentality, where there is a give and take. However, just as God does not expect his enemies to love him but still blesses them too, so also, though we cannot expect those who consider us their enemies to act lovingly toward us, we are to love them.

However, because it is so difficult to love our enemies,

many Christian teachers have excused themselves and their followers from taking this teaching of Jesus literally. This is utter dishonesty. After all, Jesus links loving our enemies with our being perfect as our Father is perfect. In other words, we can only take these words as an exaggeration if we also are willing to admit that the perfection Jesus ascribes to God is also an exaggeration. Indeed, we can only take these words to be non-literal if we also admit that the sunshine and rainfall that those who are not God's people enjoy is *not* from God.

By linking love for our enemies to God's perfection, Jesus has actually gone out of his way to ensure we do not 'spiritualize' this command. However, so corrupt are we and so desirous of vengeance that we twist even his clear words to suit our desires. But Jesus does not permit us a way to escape his demands. Those who listen to the Sermon and choose not to follow his teachings will find that they have built on sand rather than on rock. Those who do not love their enemies will discover the same. They will hear Jesus tell then that he did not know them, not because they did not call him, "Lord" or because they did not do great things by invoking his name, but precisely because, by rejecting his words in the Sermon, they demonstrated that they were aligned to a Jesus different from the one portrayed in the Sermon. And if they had aligned themselves with a different Jesus, then their relationship was with a different Jesus, not the Jesus of the Sermon on the Mount. Hence, the real Jesus, the Jesus of the Sermon truly had no relationship with them because they had turned their backs on him.

Week 13, Day 4: Spiritual exhibitionism

"Beware of practicing your righteousness before others in order to be seen by them, for then you have no reward from your Father in heaven." (Matthew 6.1)

In Matthew 6.1-18, Jesus warns us about what I would like to call 'spiritual exhibitionism'. He warns us about using the spiritual disciplines – almsgiving, prayer, and fasting – to put on a show for other so that those who see us would think highly of us. In all three cases, Jesus urges us to avoid the distractions that others introduce so that we can be wholly focused on allowing the spiritual disciplines to transform us.

Each of the disciplines is intended to strengthen our relationship with God. When we give alms, we are recognizing that whatever we have comes from God. We are also admitting that, while we may not be 'loaded', we can spare a little to help those who are worse off than we are. In doing this, we acknowledge that the welfare of other humans is more important than a slightly higher standard of living for ourselves. Also, by doing this, we weaken the grip that 'Mammon' has on us. And when we weaken its grip on us, we declare that it is a false god who cannot command our allegiance. However, when we give alms in order to receive praise from others, we, ironically, place ourselves under the thumb of Mammon because it is the giving of money that is bringing us praise from others.

In a similar way, when we pray, we are acknowledging that we are powerless and that the only one who is willing and able to help us is God himself. Prayer, therefore, is a way in which we empty ourselves of the notions that we can actually help ourselves. It is a way of accepting our finitude in the face of the enormity of the obstacles that obstruct us. However, when we pray in a way as to receive praise from others, we are actually not emptying ourselves. Rather, we are filling ourselves with the desire to be praised by others. And when we do this, we make a mockery of the discipline of prayer and render ourselves unable to be transformed by it.

Likewise, when we fast, we are admitting that humans are designed to be sustained by two sources of nourishment – food and the voice of God. Hence, when we abstain from food, we are not saying that we are starving. Rather, we are focusing ourselves on the nourishment we receive from God's voice.

Now, the two sources of nourishment are quite different in nature. Food is a tangible substance that produces powerful physiological responses in us. We feel hungry, we fill full, we feel satisfied, we feel bloated. All these physiological responses are ones that we do not need to work for apart from actually eating something when we are hungry. There is no way to avoid the effects food, or the lack of it, has on us.

God's voice, however, is intangible. Moreover, it is a 'muted' source. What I mean is that God does not overwhelm us by shouting his message into our ears or minds or hearts. Rather, he speaks by gentle persuasion in and through the mundane events of our lives as we learn to listen to him without expecting him to shout. This means that we need to make the effort to listen to him speaking to us in and through the circumstances of our lives.

However, because the other source, namely food, is so loud, the cycles we go through with respect to that source can easily drown out God's voice. Hence, when we fast, we bring that cycle to a halt or at least reduce its volume so that we can hear the quiet strains of God's voice when he speaks to us. However, if we fast in order to gain the approval of others, we add their voices to the cacophony that makes us unable to listen to God's voice. We would be rendered completely unable to hear God's voice precisely because we decided to turn our ears to the praise of others.

When we use the spiritual disciplines as ways to showcase ourselves before others, the disciplines become obstacles for us and then begin to work against us. Because of this, Jesus warns us about parading ourselves when we are engaged in the disciplines. He warns us against the ever-present snare of spiritual exhibitionism.

Week 13, Day 5: Treasures and worry

"Do not store up for yourselves treasures on earth, where moth and rust consume and where thieves break in and steal, but store up for yourselves treasures in heaven, where neither moth nor rust consumes and where thieves do not break in and steal. For where your treasure is, there your heart will be also… So do not worry about tomorrow, for tomorrow will bring worries of its own. Today's trouble is enough for today." (Matthew 6.19-21, 34)

In Matthew 6.19-34, Jesus warns us about the link between treasures and worry. Well, to be precise, he warns us about the connection between treasures on earth and worry. He speaks of the impermanence of earthly treasures. Most of us do not need to be reminded about this.

Many readers have probably invested in the stock market. However, the stock market is an entity that is completely beyond our control. We may have reasonably good powers of prediction that allow us to make sound investments most of the time. However, if the market crashes, we may find our fortunes dissolve in a day.

Many readers have probably invested in a house. While real estate prices almost always appreciate over time, there is nothing that can guarantee that the house will be standing tomorrow. A flood or an earthquake could destroy the house and cause all your dreams to come crumbling down too.

I don't think I need to cite any further examples. Life is unpredictable. And because it is unpredictable, we cannot say for certain what tomorrow will be like based on what yesterday was or what today is. In fact, what the first humans wanted when they ate from the forbidden tree is knowing before they make a decision which course of action would be best. Our desire, almost always, is to attempt to reduce the risks involved in life. This is because we treasure the things of this world, which are fleeting.

Now, don't get me wrong. I am not saying that this world is bad and that we should hate it or something like that. Quite the contrary, this world is God's good world and we should value it. However, this present creation is broken and we dare not forget it. What I am saying is that this life is inherently unpredictable and attempting to secure our futures against the unpredictability of life is not just a futile endeavor, but precisely the endeavor that gives rise to anxiety. After all, if we place before ourselves an unattainable goal, it is a perfect recipe for worry.

You see, since this world is transient, everything that belongs to this world is impermanent. However, when we invest in something in this world, we naturally develop a bond with it. And then, since we have a bond with that thing, we attempt to make it endure, often beyond its period of viability. And when we see it eventually decay, as all things in this world will, we try to hold on to it by contriving different methods of arresting the decay. But all these methods will fail because everything in this world is transient. And we begin to worry about those things when we see them spiral downward in decay.

Of course, one of the key ways in which we support the things we value is through money. Very few of us like money as an end in itself. For most of us, money is a means to different, possibly nobler, ends. However, money is based on notions of scarcity. If you receive more, there is less for me to receive. Hence, a system of value based on money is a system that survives only because it creates in us anxieties for tomorrow that we can never resolve.

Hence, Jesus tells us to form a value system based on the kingdom of heaven. That is, rather than value things that are fleeting and based on ideas of scarcity, he tells us to base our system of values on things that endure and things that can never be scarce. While he does not list any of these things, we can easily recognize that the fruit of the Spirit, which Paul

mentions in <u>Galatians 5.22-23</u>, can be the kinds of things on

which we can base our system of value. When we do this, we

begin to value things that by nature endure and that by nature

are not in limited supply. In that case, there is no room for

worry since what we value most can never be called into

question.

Week 13, Day 6: The Golden Rule, the Law, and the Prophets

Do not think that I have come to abolish the Law or the Prophets; I have come not to abolish but to fulfill… In everything do to others as you would have them do to you, for this is the Law and the Prophets. (Matthew 5.17, 7.12)

The Golden Rule has been stated by people other than Jesus too. Some Christians attempt to elevate Jesus over the others by claiming that Jesus said it in a positive sense (i.e. 'do') rather than in a negative sense (i.e. 'do not') or in an inverted sense (i.e. 'what you want others to do for you, you should do for them'). However, this tendency undermines Jesus' words. We should be as gracious as possible to everyone who has concluded anything that would lead to something like the Golden Rule.

What sets Jesus apart is not his recognition that people should treat others in a manner in which they like to be treated. That is simply something that any human knows in their bones. When someone says, "That's unfair," they are simply saying that the other person has not treated them in a way that person would want to be treated. Of course, we are quick to recognize instances when we face injustice rather than instances when we are perpetrators of injustice.

What sets Jesus apart, especially in the context of Jewish religious thought, is his linking of the idea of not abolishing the Law and the Prophets with the idea that the Law and the Prophets were about the Golden Rule. Of course, this should shock us, if we are honest. The Old Testament has many parts that are not quite aligned with the Golden Rule. There are commands to commit genocide. There are laws that prescribe the death penalty for all sorts of minor misdemeanors. There is no place for forgiveness for major offences. And there is a decided 'insider-outsider' mentality. In light of this, how can Jesus say that he did not come to abolish the Law and the Prophets and that the Law and the Prophets were about the Golden Rule?

We must disabuse ourselves of the notion that the bible is a book of instructions. I was fortunately quite well into my serious attempt at following Jesus when I first heard the abominable acronym 'Basic Instructions Before Leaving Earth' (i.e. BIBLE). I have been a teacher for quite a few years now. And I know that the goal of a teacher is to make himself/herself redundant. That is, I have succeeded as a teacher when my students have understood what I have taught so well that they do not need to remain in my tutelage. Then, they can move from being my students to becoming my friends, as Jesus tells his disciples in John 15.15. The goal of a teacher, if the teacher is like Jesus, is to make friends.

However, friends are those for whom we are responsible and from whom we can expect responsibility. That is, in a relationship of friendship, there is a mutuality of responsibility, one for the other. When we consider the bible to be a book on instructions that we must repeatedly consult for guidance, we are saying that we refuse to move to becoming Jesus' friends, that is, those he can count on to be responsible. What do I mean?

When we see Jesus in the Sermon on the Mount, he is often interacting with parts of the Old Testament. For instance, when he says, "You have heard it said… but I say to you," these are the results of deep reflection on those parts of the Old Testament. What he tells us is that the Old Testament is not to be taken as instructions that need to be followed blindly. Rather, we need to filter the Old Testament through the lens of the Golden Rule and reflect on the alignments and the misalignments.

For instance, Jesus reflects on the commandment about adultery and says that it is not stringent enough since it addresses only the outward action even though adultery begins in the heart. However, when it comes to the law of retaliation (i.e. 'eye for an eye, tooth for a tooth'), he completely rejects it in place of nonviolent direct action. In both cases, whether making one command stricter or rejecting another, Jesus reveals that he has treated the Old Testament as meditation literature, that is literature that needed to be reflected upon rather than blindly adhered to.

What Jesus tells us through the Golden Rule is that we should read the Law and the Prophets as though the shoe were on the other foot. If this reversal of roles makes us uncomfortable, then perhaps the commandment does not pass the Golden Rule test and should be amended or rejected. This is not an abolishment of the Law and the Prophets because they provide us with the context for our wrestling. In other words, if we take the role of the Law and the Prophets to be that of giving us contexts for wrestling with the purposes and character of God, then even if we reject a commandment here or amend another there, since it is the Law and the Prophets that have given us the opportunity to undertake this wrestling, we have not abolished their continued relevance in our lives.

Week 13, Day 7: Faith, obedience, and discipleship

Enter through the narrow gate, for the gate is wide and the road is easy that leads to destruction, and there are many who take it. For the gate is narrow and the road is hard that leads to life, and there are few who find it… Everyone, then, who hears these words of mine and acts on them will be like a wise man who built his house on rock… And everyone who hears these words of mine and does not act on them will be like a foolish man who built his house on sand. (Matthew 7.13-14, 24, 26)

Throughout the Sermon on the Mount, Jesus is consistent about the non-negotiable nature of faith and obedience for discipleship. Not only does he not even entertain the possibility of a disjunction between the two, as Paul and James do in their letters, but also, he makes it clear that any thought that there could be a disjunction indicates that a person is not actually his disciple.

Of course, if we are thinking that discipleship to Jesus is a criterion for 'salvation', especially if this 'salvation' is construed as an escape from some never-ending punishment, then what Jesus says makes no sense. After all, then we cannot avoid the conclusion that what we do is at least a part of the criteria on which the decision to send us to punishment or not is made. If this is the case, then what Jesus teaches can *never* be taken as words of comfort and assurance. Rather, his words themselves would be the cause for anxiety and worry since we would never know if we are doing the right things all the time and certainly not if we are doing them with the right motives. In that case, Jesus' teachings become millstones around our necks.

The only way out of this artificial and self-imposed quandary is to reject the idea that Jesus is teaching anything about a never-ending punishment. A never-ending punishment, after all is punishment for its own sake, punishment with no purpose other than inflicting pain on someone else. Nothing, I repeat, nothing in Jesus' life ever indicates that he ever considered punishment of this kind to be worthy of himself or worthy of his Father. Rather, he seemed to always indicate a desire for a restoration of relationship between estranged humans and their Father.

If this is the case, then Jesus' words of warning in the Sermon on the Mount cannot be construed as being warnings about never-ending punishment. Therefore, the very idea that there is a 'salvation' that involves an escape from a never-ending punishment is not something that Jesus ever taught.

With this realization we can understand that Jesus' words about the narrow and wide gates have no relevance for what happens to us after we die. Rather, this is about discipleship in the here and now. Following Jesus' teachings is the narrow gate not because few people are saved but because few people are willing to wholeheartedly accept the restrictions he places on his disciples. Indeed, precisely because his demands on his disciples are so constricting, most of those who identify as his disciples are those who are counted among the many who choose the wide gate because they have excused themselves from the difficult task of following him.

But you, the reader, know better. In these devotions I have consistently allowed Jesus' high demands to speak for themselves. I have not allowed conventional wisdom or traditional Christian teachings to water down what he told us in and through the Sermon on the Mount. Rather, you have had a sustained thirteen-week immersion into the wellspring that is the life to which Jesus calls *all* his disciples. It is a difficult road he calls us to walk. It is not difficult because we face opposition from others, though that may be the case for many of us. Rather, it is difficult because Jesus himself proscribes certain courses of action. After all, when he says, "Love your enemies," he does not allow us a place to nurture hate. And when he utters the Golden Rule, he tells us that empathy is the defining quality of his disciples, on account of which they are able to have a dynamic way of approaching the scriptures that always elevates the wellbeing of others above any determination to follow scripture legalistically.

And so, having completed this set of devotions, I hope you are better prepared to weather the storms that will surely come in your life. And may you always find your identity, in the midst of these storms, built upon the rock of obedience to Jesus.

www.ingramcontent.com/pod-product-compliance
Lightning Source LLC
Chambersburg PA
CBHW041302120726

48005CB00014B/1826